DIGITAL PR

PRCA PRACTICE GUIDES

DIGITAL PR

BY

DANNY WHATMOUGH

United Kingdom – North America – Japan – India
Malaysia – China

Emerald Publishing Limited
Howard House, Wagon Lane, Bingley BD16 1WA, UK

First edition 2019

Reprints and permissions service
Contact: permissions@emeraldinsight.com

British Library Cataloguing in Publication Data
A catalogue record for this book is available from the British
Library

ISBN: 978-1-78756-622-4
ISBN: 978-1-78756-619-4 (E-ISBN)
ISBN: 978-1-78756-621-7 (Epub)

ISOQAR certified
Management System,
awarded to Emerald
for adherence to
Environmental
standard
ISO 14001:2004.

ISOQAR
REGISTERED

Certificate Number 1985
ISO 14001

INVESTOR IN PEOPLE

For Mum, Rachel and Marla

CONTENTS

FOREWORD

PRCA Practice Guides are a series of uniquely practical and readable guides, providing PR and communications professionals, new and experienced alike, with hands-on guidance to manage in the field. Written by experienced practitioners who have been there and done it, the books in the series offer powerful insights into the challenges of the modern industry and guidance on how to navigate your way through them.

Most people will agree that digital has been a game-changer in marketing and PR. At a time when no-one has all the answers, this book will help PR and communications professionals to understand the areas they need to consider using in digital communications, and the questions they need to ask in order to excel in this new digital age. This book charts the progress of digital PR – where we've come from, where we are now, and where we are going. It mixes practical advice and tips to guide the modern PR practitioner. It isn't designed for digital specialists but those working in the PR industry that need to ensure they are on the right path. It contains thoughts and opinions from someone working at the forefront of the industry and helping to shape its future.

Danny Whatmough is a senior professional who has unparalleled experience in digital and social media for PR and communications. He is currently Managing Director, EVP,

Integrated Media at Weber Shandwick and previously headed up social and digital for Proctor & Gamble at Ketchum. He is currently Chairman of the PRCA's Digital Group, a member of the PRCA PR and Communications Council, and sits on the AMEC social media measurement committee. Such is the level of his digital expertise that he was handed the Outstanding Contribution award at the PRCA Digital Awards 2018. Indeed, he plays an active role in the wider PR industry and is a regular speaker, commentator, and blogger on digital PR and the future of the industry.

Francis Ingham
Director General, PRCA
Chief Executive, ICCO

1

INTRODUCTION

There is no such thing as 'digital'. That might seem an odd first sentence in a book about digital Public Relations (PR). However, the reality is that digital is so pervasive in our daily lives that the sheer task of trying to divorce it from what is not digital is fruitless.

Let us think about this in a more tangible way. If you receive a piece of media coverage in a national newspaper, there is no doubt these days that the coverage will also appear on the newspaper's website. Therefore, is that digital PR or not? It is both and neither.

This conundrum is a tricky one when approaching a book on the subject. Thus, rather than trying to define what exactly digital PR is or isn't – a purely academic or semantic exercise with little profit – I am instead trying to approach this more in a way that gives a sense of how digital technology has caused a shift in the PR profession.

What are the strategic approaches and tactics that the digital age has ushered in? What are the ways in which organisations and businesses have had to change the way they talk to their audiences? In addition, what are the new skill sets and training we need as practitioners as a result?

AN INDUSTRY SLOW TO ADAPT

The criticism of the PR industry has often been that it is slow
to adapt to changing technological developments. There is
perhaps a fair amount of truth in this critique. I genuinely
believe the PR industry failed to see the opportunity that
search engine marketing – and Search Engine Optimisation
(SEO), in particular – offered. As a whole, the industry did
not see or respond to the potential of SEO and it did not bring
in specialists who could meaningfully create a new offering.

Of course, it is easy to taint a whole industry with one brush.
The reality is that some have adapted quickly and benefitted
as a result. It is also easy to be hard on yourself. In addition,
the reality is that many industries have struggled with digitisation. Moreover, many of our sister disciplines within the marketing sphere have had similar challenges when it comes to the
adoption of digital – and social media, in particular.

NEEDED NOW MORE THAN EVER

Therefore, just as it is impossible to divorce digital from 'not
digital' in a communications industry sense, it is also impossible to divorce digital from the world in general.

Over the last 15 years or so, the digitisation of the world
at large has been rapid and disruptive. The evidence of it is
everywhere. How could we have predicted being able to pay
for goods in a shop using our watch? Could we have foreseen
hailing a taxi through a mobile device? Would it have been
possible to anticipate ordering a product and having it arrive
at your doorstep within two hours?

There is no industry or person on this earth that has not
been impacted by this phenomenon. Therefore, what is the
role for communications within this environment?

It is easy to look at the disruption in our industry, but it is actually the disruption in consumer consumption that we need to focus on, which will be a major theme of this book, starting with a look at the use of data in Chapter 2.

Where disruption reigns, communication becomes more and more important. The innate human desire to make sense of things requires clear and consistent communication to bring clarity and comfort. There will be no slowing of the pace of change. The next 15 years will make the last 15 look tame; and on, and on.

SOCIETAL SHIFTS

Society has been confronted with some major challenges driven in part by technological advances. Trust in large organisations, businesses and public figures is at an all-time low. Much of this is due to a lack of effective communication.

We live in a time when consumers have unparalleled power. They can find information out more easily than ever before. They can contact those in authority in a very public way and, should these attempts fail, they can make their displeasure felt for the whole world to see. These public comments are always just a few retweets away from viral sensation.

This has brought forth a whole array of ethical considerations. A clarion call for transparency has been the biggest defining communication shift in the past decade. In addition, it has signalled a move away from PR spin across the board. From the world of politics to that of celebrity and business, the masks have, and are still, being torn down. Those that have anticipated this and changed their relationship with their publics have survived. Those that have not, have felt the full power of public pressure.

Of course, this has also spurred debate and discussion around privacy – or lack of privacy. In addition, this is not something that just affects the rich and famous, but hits at an individual level too.

TRUST AND THE DECLINE OF THE THIRD ESTATE

Many have started to use these shifts to their advantage. At the same time as the move towards a more transparent way of acting, others have used this trend to create their own untruths and embraced self-publishing technologies, such as social networks, to reach mass audiences and alter global power structures.

This has been driven by – and has contributed to – an erosion of the established media. There are a number of factors at play here, but central to a lot of what has happened has been distribution. The analogue approach to the distribution of news was something that worked well for the publisher business model. Newspapers controlled their 'product' and could therefore control everything around it, from the price you paid to consume to the adverts you saw on the printed page.

The web changed everything. Distribution was unbundled. Advertising became ubiquitous and therefore diminished in value. As social networks (which were never originally intended to be a source for news) started to offer new opportunities, publishers were sceptical and reluctant participants in the inevitable shift. Now, vast swathes of people get their news from social media every day. In addition, far more telling, despite the fact that most people can remember the social platform where they encountered a piece of news, only 47% can remember the publisher brand that served them the piece of content (Reuters Institute, 2017).

Those that want to manipulate the public have used this to their advantage. At a time when the traditional media are losing their power and authority – for all the reasons presented thus far – the void that opens up is easily filled.

MASS INFLUENCE IS WITHIN REACH

Witness the rise of the influencer. It has always been true that we are each able to influence those around us. However, the web has brought the potential of mass influence to each one of us. We live in an age where a teenage girl, broadcasting from her bedroom, can amass an audience big enough to prompt a cosmetic product to sell out. We live in an age when teenagers from Macedonia can write a totally fake news story about a US Presidential candidate that helps influence a democratic election.

Gone are the checks, the balances and the rigour that governed and self-governed professional news organisations. It is painful to see established and respected news organisations being reduced to click-farms catering to the lowest common denominator in a race for eyeballs. Moreover, it is scary to see how 'fake news' can be used as a critique as well as a justification of a viewpoint – whether true or not.

Shifts in consumer consumption mean this is a societal issue that will only increase, due in large part to sophisticated use of data. The filter bubble is a concept that is not actually that new, but has come into modern vernacular because of the 2016 US Presidential Election and the Brexit referendum of the same year in the United Kingdom. In the past, we would create a filter bubble of sorts by selecting a certain daily newspaper over another. Today, filter bubbles mean that we can end up only being exposed to information and 'news' that meets our selective worldview. Moreover, these articles can be from respected sources or not.

THE DEATH OF INTERRUPTION MARKETING

Moreover, as we will see throughout this book, traditional marketing has not been immune to these shifts either. Consumers are voting with their eyeballs. Marketing communications that interrupt an experience are being rejected, even if many platforms are still pursuing advertising products in this domain.

Content marketing is often touted as the solution to this problem; however, the endless challenge here is that the content itself needs to be good enough to stand out in a world where information (and content) overload is a problem that is growing exponentially.

There is a creative opportunity here – the content needs to be better to cut through and, in an era of information overload, it is only the best content that will win. Of course, it has to be delivered in the right way, which is why the success of digital ad formats like display are plummeting in effectiveness. Earned media has a powerful role to play in this new content ecosystem.

THE DIGITAL STATUS QUO

It is easy to be downbeat by all of this. The truth is that this is an evolution of the environment we currently find ourselves in and new norms will be established, ready for disruption by the next macro shift.

The reason for walking through some of these trends is to set a backdrop against which modern PR exists. As communicators and consultants, we have a professional duty to help businesses and organisations navigate these choppy waters, not only to help them communicate to their publics in the best possible light, but also to ensure that they uphold ethical responsibilities around transparency and authenticity.

At a time when 140 characters (or even 280) can cause share prices to plummet, the need for agile, responsive PR is pivotal.

As the above discussion hopefully proves, and as I shall continue to argue through this book, there is not an opt-out for digital PR. Digital is not a silo; it is the status quo. It is a reality of the world and industry in which we work. An understanding of the challenges and opportunities that digital presents is the only way to safeguard our industry and the work we do for the businesses and organisations we work for and with.

TOWARDS AN EVOLVED APPROACH

Therefore, in conclusion, it is probably easier to tell you what this book is not. It is not a how-to guide. It is not a manual. What it does, is look at the changes digital technology has ushered in, giving some ideas or recommendations for how to proceed if you have not already, or question again if it is something you've already tackled. Every chapter ends with a series of questions to ponder – things that might spark new ideas or new ways of looking at a problem.

The final thing to note before we begin is that, as with all things digital, this book will be out of date before it is even published. Therefore, where possible, I have tried not to focus on specific technologies or applications. I prefer to talk about broader trends or approaches that will still be relevant in the years to come, even if the way they are used are things that we just would not be able to predict, even if we wanted to.

THE MORE THINGS CHANGE, THE MORE THINGS STAY THE SAME

It would be easy to summarise this book as being all about change. However, it is really about evolution. Although digital has changed the day-to-day activities of most PR practitioners in terms of what they tactically do, most of the theory and strategy around constructing a PR approach has stayed surprisingly constant.

Therefore, as we talk about the future and the cutting edge, let us not throw the baby out with the bathwater and remember that effective communication with a brand or organisation's publics is still the number one goal and something that we as an industry should continue to uphold.

2

DATA

This chapter is deliberately first in this book. For me, access to data has been the biggest shift in the PR industry over the last few years and yet, perhaps, the one area that has been most overlooked.

There are many reasons for this but the availability of accurate data is probably key. Added to this is the fact that, although the data exists to better inform PR approaches, collecting this data and pulling them together in the right way still are not easy and require new skill sets. There is plenty of work to be done in this area and technology providers have a big role to play; but, nevertheless, there is a wealth of opportunity available right now and that is what we will explore here in more detail.

This chapter deliberately avoids a detailed exploration of measurement and reporting – something that is obviously crucial to any discussion around data. There is a dedicated chapter on this very subject, later in the book. This is because, firstly, the topic warrants its own space for a more detailed analysis and, secondly, because I think it is useful to see planning and reporting as separate disciplines, albeit very closely linked, both with data at their core.

THE ROLE FOR DATA IN PR

Data has always been on the fringes of traditional PR practice. Yes, we have collected data for measurement and reporting but these have often been shallow metrics with limited practical insight (more of this in the reporting chapter 11). Yes, we have often used data for storytelling, whether owned data or the third-party research that has been commissioned. Yes, we have used data to inform media targeting and distribution, but again, it has never been subjected to the rigour that you would find in other marketing disciplines.

This lack of depth is due largely to access. Moreover, this lack of access means that PR has developed with a subjective rather than objective mindset. Often, decisions about which publications to give an embargo to, or the best influencer to use for a campaign have been based on the knowledge of the media or influencer ecosystem by the individual or team of professionals. There is nothing wrong with this. Long-held knowledge and experience, built up over a period through trial and error, is something that cannot be easily taught. It is a natural skill and one that is of significant value to businesses and organisations.

An individual's worth in this industry has often been reduced to the might of her 'little black book' – again, nothing wrong with this from a relationship standpoint but it is not the most objective, data-led approach, either.

Data does not necessarily negate this need either. It can enhance and support, bringing forth new opportunities or helping to convince senior stakeholders of the right approach to take.

GETTING DATA ACCESS

The internet has changed the rules when it comes to access to data. It is the old cliché that, with digital, everything is measureable. Moreover, it is true, to a point. Suddenly, as consumer consumption behaviour has shifted to the web, we have a mountain of information on who is reading what, where and when.

In addition, the good news is, slowly but surely, we are beginning to get access to this data – often, for free.

Social networks are a good case in point here. Jump into the advertising planning tools of any of the major platforms and you will get access to wealth of information – supposedly, to be used for paid media activities, but just as useful for earned insights. (The URLs change but searching for 'Facebook/Twitter ad planner' should give you the result you need.)

More traditional sources of data are possible, too. Moreover, here, we must look to the methods employed by some of our sisters in the marketing industry – principally the media agency. Tools such as TGI and, more latterly, Global Web Index – are able to provide access to macro consumption trends. They can tell you whether a specific demographic is consuming certain types of media and what device they are using to do it.

Therefore, as we begin to navigate this digital media environment, data is vital. As we will see in Chapter 3, the digital ecosystems that we are now operating within are more complex than ever before. There are more channels and a myriad of different ways to use them. There are also many different entry points to access information. Someone accessing your website via their mobile device will very probably be looking for a different answer – or at least experience – than someone browsing via a laptop. Data has the power to tell us who is who and when we get it right (and when we do not).

It is also important to note that the use of data is not just something that is being embraced in other marketing disciplines. It is also an area where media publishers are leading the charge. If you look at some of the new digital publishers out there – Buzzfeed is the obvious example – you will quickly find that their use of data is fundamental to their success.

As Jonah Peretti, chief executive officer of Buzzfeed says,

> *What is the competitive advantage that you can gain as a publisher today? You're not going to inherit one or get one given to you by a spectrum grant. Having technology, data science, and being able to know how to manage, optimize, and coordinate your publishing is the thing that gives you a competitive advantage (Fast Company, 2016).*

Therefore, this chapter will focus on how a digital PR approach needs to start with data and then use this as a running leitmotif through campaign and execution – right the way through to measurement – to ensure that a clear strategy is put in place, content is created in the right way and distribution hits the nail on the head. Let us start with audiences.

UNDERSTANDING AUDIENCES

Of course, as alluded to in Chapter 1, access to data is pretty powerful but, as with all data analysis, it has to be focussed in the right direction; otherwise, it just becomes a sea of numbers. Moreover, from a planning standpoint, that means focussing on audiences.

Knowing who it is that you are trying to reach seems like a very obvious thing, but I'm constantly amazed at how many businesses fail to have a clear understanding of exactly who it is they are trying to speak or sell to. If there is one thing that is critical to the success of any campaign, then this is it.

There are a number of different approaches to build audience profiles or segmentations. Moreover, there are various schools of thought on the relative merits of different approaches. It is highly likely that the process of building audience segmentations will not always fall to the PR professional (although no reason why PR practitioners should not lead in this regard). No matter how this information manifests itself, as full-blown personas or demographic one pagers, it is safe to say that there are a number of questions that, from a PR perspective, would need to be answered by any audience analysis:

- What is the average demographic information of the target audience (e.g. gender and age)?

- What are their media consumption habits (e.g. newspapers, magazines, TV and advertising)?

- What are their device or channel usage habits (e.g. internet, mobile and offline)?

- Who/what influences them (e.g. individuals and media)?

- What topics do they follow (e.g. themes, trends, macro – politics, film – and/or specific – Brexit, Romcoms)?

- How interested are they in your business/organisation/ product or service?

- Do they interact with your competitors more or less than you?

These are not comprehensive and they are not specific. Yours should be and they will change from business to business and from campaign to campaign. However, the above mentioned pointers are a good start and should hopefully provoke further thought.

It is important to note at this point that any business or organisation will rarely just have the one audience. They are likely to have many. This is a marketing challenge that digital has a solution to like no other. In the analogue PR world, you could target different publications to speak to a different audience. It is a crude but possible approach. But what happens when you want to use a broad reach publication like a national newspaper? How do you cater your message to an investor audience and a consumer audience all through the same vehicle? It is very difficult and always, at best, a blunt instrument. However, with digital PR and precise targeting – as we will discover, it is now possible. However, you need the data to inform and deliver this type of approach.

It is also important to point out that, if audience segmentations have been undertaken within the business itself or by the marketing side of the business, then they will probably focus primarily on the prime consumers of the product and service.

With PR, in particular, we should always remember the broader audiences that we often need to think about – for example, partners, suppliers, employees, political stakeholders, industry influencers, etc. In many ways, these audiences are just as important for our digital PR approach (as we will see later) and the more information and data we can have on them at this early stage, the better.

Accessing data that will help you answer the questions above should be relatively easy. However, it will also likely be from a combination of sources. Many businesses these days will hold reams of information that will prove useful in compiling your audience viewpoint. Some of the data will be from the business itself but third-party data – especially for verification – is likely to be invaluable. Industry reports and benchmarks allow you to ground what you have into something more contextual. Comparing multiple data sources and finding commonalities will also be useful. Having analysts that can help you gather and then process this information will be invaluable.

Finally, before we move away from audiences, it is important to note that this data will change over time. Audience analysis and segmentation is not a job that can be done once and then archived. Audience behaviour is changing faster than ever. Therefore, find ways to ensure this is being updated on a regular basis. There is nothing worse than receiving an audience segmentation that is more than two years old. Today, some of the social networks that audiences are using might not even have been in existence two years ago!

PUTTING DATA THROUGH A BUSINESS LENS

Audience insights are absolutely critical; however, it is also important not to forget the role of the business or organisation. Moreover, that is where we begin to build out the audience information gathered into more of a strategic PR or communication approach, based on data.

Taking each audience in turn, you can then begin to answer some key strategic questions:

1. How relatively important is this audience for us as a business?

2. What are the best channels for us to reach them?

3. What is the best approach for communication (e.g. direct interaction, via third parties – media, influencers, via paid advertising and combinations of the above)?

4. What is the intersection between the topics they are interested in and that we have a right to talk about?

This is a crucial jumping off point as we start to pull together a channel ecosystem and customer journey. It is something that we will consider in far more detail in Chapter 3; however, for now, it is just important to remember how to access the information and the insights that it can bring as a result.

It is clear to see how this will then feed into content planning, strategy and creative. Topic analysis is a great way to start and a good strategist will find not only those areas where there is significant audience interest, but also a lack of competitive content or information out there already. It is also helpful to look at how content trends change over time. A clear example of this is the simple, free tool that Google created to analyse search trends. Google Trends can be a great way to get a macro-picture of how certain topics fluctuate in the public zeitgeist. It is also fascinating to see how the traditional media are often a key trigger for search volumes spiking.

DATA AND ITS ROLE IN TARGETING

So far, we have seen how data can aid the planning process through detailed insights into the target audience and how they consume information or how they are influenced. Data, in this context, is something that we will revisit throughout this book.

But once we get into the detail of planning a campaign or piece of PR activity, data has a much more active role to play. It's not just something that can be used as the bookends to a campaign.

Targeting – as has been alluded to already – is vitally important here. The information that we have gathered about our audiences gives us vital clues as to how and where they consume information. This not only feeds directly into our strategic approach, but also into the way we create and build content.

However, the data collected will be just as – if not more – important when it comes to distribution. This could be as simple as informing us which publications (and even which journalists at those publications) would be worth us considering for campaign outreach. Using techniques such as conversation analysis, it is possible to conduct a detailed investigation into where particular topics are being discussed and which are the journalists writing these pieces and the influencers being quoted in them. In the past, this would have involved significant manual involvement; however, today, it is something that can be done with relative ease through the use of technology.

TARGETING ON STEROIDS THROUGH SOCIAL

In the social space, this becomes far more sophisticated very quickly. Most people will be familiar with some of the more obvious uses of demographic information when targeting audiences through paid activity on social networks. Selecting someone's age, gender and location immediately gives you a clear picture of how to target a specific audience. You can then use more qualitative data to further narrow this down – for example, if people follow a particular brand or belong to a certain group.

This wipes the floor with anything that was possible with older forms of media targeting. However, it does not stop there. The social targeting discussed earlier is all using data that has been collected by the networks themselves. Twitter, but particularly Facebook, will collect significant demographic information about you that can be used by marketers in targeting in this way. But, using first- and third-party data, combined with the data the networks hold, you can be far more specific and efficient with the way you are targeting:

- *First-party data* – Social channels now allow you to upload information you hold as a business to help you target relevant people through paid media. Therefore, for example, you could upload a current customer or prospect list. In a secure way, the networks 'hash' the data so that it stays anonymous. They then match the data you upload – for example, email addresses or telephone numbers – with the data they have on their users. This then allows you to create very specific targeting lists – you can then append the other information already discussed.

- *Platform data* – Social and digital platforms are constantly collecting data on us based on the information we share with the platform in question. This can be everything from demographic information to insights around preferences – for example, the accounts we connect with or the content we 'like'.

- *Third-party data* – Another interesting data source that is increasingly being used for targeting is third-party data vendors. Most of the major social networks have partnered with one or more of these companies and they provide data insight that you would not hold as a business and that the networks would not receive from their audiences during the course of their use of the platform. The information provided varies significantly but the depth of it is quite staggering, with some companies claiming to have hundreds and hundreds of data points on individuals. This can range from things like purchase history, to the size or your house or when you last purchased a car.

These three data sources are significant and again another reason why social media are becoming such a powerful marketing tool. Most platforms also give you the opportunity to use a technique called 'lookalike audiences' where you can use the data profiling opportunities that platforms hold to find other people that have a similar 'footprint' to the audience that you've identified. This becomes a very important tactic for media pitching as well as for social media engagement and paid media activities, as we will see in later chapters 4, 5 and 9.

Obviously, all the above depends on content having paid media support (which is pretty much vital for all social media activity anyway these days, as we will see in the chapter 5 on social media) but there are obviously organic data points, too, during the course of a campaign. You can use data such as who engaged with content – whether through likes, comments or shares. You can identify if someone clicked through to your website and what they did as a result.

The last point here underpins the importance of owned properties and the data contained there. For many organisations, a website is still an important tool in any campaign and thus the metrics that you receive are not just important for measurement, they are important for the optimisation of a campaign, too.

TESTING AND LEARNING

We have talked a little bit already about agility during a campaign and hopefully, by now, it is clear to see the role that data can play. There are watch-outs here. With so much data available, it is easy to be lulled into a state of inertia. Choosing the right Key Performance Indicator (KPIs) and keeping track of the right metrics will ensure that informed decisions can be made during a campaign.

However, for this to work, agility and real-time data collection are absolutely vital. Dashboards are a great solution to data overload. Providing a clear snapshot of what is going on at any particular point in time will provide clear ways to make informed decisions on the fly. In an ideal world, these dashboards are real-time – or as near to – and, in a world in which multi-channel is the new norm, dashboards should collate and match data from different sources – channel and business metrics – so that patterns can be detected and meaningful insights drawn.

Agility with ongoing data analysis is also about responsibility. I have seen many cases where all-singing-all-dancing dashboards are created, only for them to sit alone, unviewed by human eyes. There must be a reason for them to exist and a desire to use their insights to improve a campaign; otherwise, nothing will happen.

REACTIVE DATA INSIGHTS

So far, we have focussed a lot on using data to inform proactive campaign planning. Data is great when you have time to analyse and digest. However, it can also be used in fast turnaround situations. Newsjacking is nothing new for PR professionals. It is a tried and tested tactic of news generation. To date, scouring the daily papers or trying to predict big events in the near future was the extent to which analysis entered the picture. However, data provides opportunities to super-charge this reactive approach.

Social listening is a key vehicle here and a powerful way to see exactly what topics of conversation are spiking. However, it is also possible these days to identify topics *before* they hit the mainstream. This will allow us to predict where the next big trend will come from and provide time to craft a response that will gain cut through.

Of course, reactive data doesn't just help for news generation; it also has an important role to play in crisis communication. Being able to identify where potentially damaging conversations are taking place and how to manage them is something that data analysis and listening has made far easier – even though the number of conversations has multiplied. Obviously, this is easy to do through social channels. However, conversation analysis can now take place across all media sources, something that makes old-school clipping services look clunky. We will look at digital crisis communication in a lot more detail later and data will be at the heart of that approach, too.

BUILDING A DATA OPERATION

As I said at the start, for me, data is the single biggest shift that the PR industry has experienced. However, most practitioners have yet to really embrace the opportunity. Again, as remarked on earlier, there is a good reason for this. Access to data is one thing but access to relevant skill sets is another. There are many hurdles here and financing an effective data-led approach is probably at the forefront. However, the investment in data and the tools and people that can analyse it, will pay dividends later.

It is also important to reflect that, as the technology gets smarter, a lot of this can now start to be automated. We have touched on dashboards as a good example of this, but technologies like artificial intelligence mean that long manual analysis can often be cut out significantly, if not entirely, through building scripts to automate simple processes.

It is hard to overestimate the importance of data in our industry. We will talk in more depth later about the role of measurement – and this is another area where the PR industry has been negligent in the past. Data can be transformational and lead to insights that not only create campaigns that are closer to the audiences they are trying to reach, but also can ensure that, when executed, these campaigns are continually optimised and work in the way they were intended.

QUESTIONS

1. What data is useful for your strategic approach?

2. How are you going to get access to this data?

3. Do you know who you are looking to reach with a piece of activity?

4. How do you uncover real data insights about your audience and how to reach them?

5. What is the role that data is going to play through your campaign from start to finish?

6. Are you revisiting your data on a regular basis to ensure it is still relevant and up-to-date?

7. Are you looking at macro trends over time?

8. What data is available to help you target the right audience in the right place at the right time?

9. What first- and third-party data sources are available for you to use? How are you using platform data?

10. How are you presenting data and information? Could dashboards offer a real-time solution?

3

THE DIGITAL PR ECOSYSTEM

The theme of complexity continues when we turn our attention to the PR ecosystem. In the past, it was relatively straight-forward – the media (and potentially some other influencers) were our main 'channel', the main way by which we would reach an audience. Much of this was due to ease. It just was not possible to reach an audience in an earned way directly, en masse. Word of mouth was clearly possible but the media were the trigger, the mouthpiece.

As we have seen, the digital revolution has changed all of that. The ability to reach anyone, directly, through the web has unparalleled implications for us as PR practitioners. It brings an incredible opportunity, but brings some headaches too. The channels at our disposal are now limitless.

So much of the work of PR professionals is so closely tied (traditionally, at least) with the media. Moreover, the media is a sector that has come under more pressure and challenges due to digital. At the same time, both industries – PR and media – have been radically altered beyond recognition with changing consumer behaviours when it comes to the consumption of information.

Against this backdrop, it is not hard to see how the PR industry has often struggled to know which way to turn. The advent of search marketing was a massive opportunity missed. Nevertheless, there were significant challenges here, not least the need for significant technical knowledge that just was not around in the industry. Some agencies have thrived by offering SEO services through partnership or acquisition, but this is not necessarily a quick and easy solution.

Social has been a much more fruitful hunting ground and is a natural bedfellow for the PR professional. In fact, my first real reason for entering the PR industry was because I felt it was the natural place for social communication to reside within the marketing ecosystem.

THE SOCIAL SHIFT

Yet, this was in many ways a naive outlook. Of course, social media is an area where the PR industry has seized the opportunity and made significant inroads. However, PR does not 'own' social media in the way that it 'owned' traditional media relations within a brand or an organisation. The technologies that power social media or digital PR in general are now all pervasive across a business or organisation.

The HR team has a powerful right to use social for recruitment. The marketing team will be adept at using the direct marketing capabilities of Facebook and product development teams will want a piece of the pie when it comes to mining social conversations for predictive product trends.

Therefore, as we will talk about later, the ubiquity of these technologies and their all-encompassing nature not only bring challenges for businesses and organisations, but also to those working within PR agencies or departments.

HOMOGENISED MARKETING

Which brings us to another trend that we will revisit throughout this book – that of homogenised marketing. The shift to integrated marketing has been a long time coming. In fact, it should have already been and gone, except for the silos that we construct within businesses that like to keep things in their boxes.

It takes an individual that is sure in her capabilities and knowledge to push true integration – especially, when that person sits within an agency. However, the reality is that, the more you push the boundaries of what is possible through an evolved, digital approach to PR, the more you are forced to integrate with other disciplines, other practitioners and other partners.

There is a structural issue here too for agencies and in-house teams – where the need to bring in new skill sets is a constant challenge – especially, for smaller teams. Knowing when to invest and when to partner or integrate is key and we'll tackle this in chapter 13.

DEFINING WHAT SUCCESS LOOKS LIKE

Therefore, as we begin to consider our new ecosystem, it is important to do it in a focussed way. We cannot use every channel for every business, client or campaign and neither should we.

We are often our own worst enemy here, though. So often, a brilliantly thought-through integrated PR strategy, which blends elements of multi-channel thinking, has been ruined in execution by defaulting back to an expectation that everything will drive coverage. We will talk in a lot more detail later about the struggle between outcomes and outputs but, for me, the biggest barrier to truly effective digital and integrated PR thinking is a focus on outputs. The yearly coverage target is the bluntest of blunt instruments and immediately quashes integrated thinking.

Again, as we will see later, outputs definitely have their place, but not in planning. Here, we need to focus on the outcomes we want and these have to be aligned to marketing and business objectives.

Then, we take the data and insights that we discussed in Chapter 2 and begin to define an ecosystem that works for an audiences and meets the specific objectives that have been defined.

THE QUESTION OF OWNERSHIP

This is when the departmental or agency bun-fight usually commences. In addition, generally speaking, the larger the business, the harder true integration becomes (though I have seen notable exceptions to this rule at both ends of the spectrum).

True marcomms planning should occur without any of these tribal complications. I appreciate that is far easier said than done, and I can probably count the instances through my career to date on one hand. Therefore, at worst, this should be a collaborative effort that arrives at a point that has consensus on all sides. A true understanding of the audience and the business or campaign objectives is the only effective starting place and everything else should then stem from there.

In smaller businesses where multi-departmental or multi-agency environments are not commonplace, life should be easier. However, the counter-balance here is that often planning is not subjected to the same scrutiny and that can be an issue too.

CONSTRUCTING THE CUSTOMER JOURNEY

Terminology often becomes a stumbling block in strategy and planning. It seems every marketing or comms director and, certainly, every agency has its own process and verbiage that comes with it. This is unfortunate as it gets in the way of what should be a fairly straightforward process with clear and concise outputs.

In an ideal world, the following are the ideal outputs from a planning process:

- *Objectives* – There should be clear recognition of what everyone is pushing to achieve. There should really only be one core objective in an ideal world but there might be some sub-objectives, too. This should be the north star and never alter.

- *Audience definitions and insights* – Sometimes called personas, it is important that everyone is using the same definition of the target audience. This should not only include information of who they are from a demographic and ideally psychographic standpoint, but also the channel and behavioural information. As mentioned in Chapter 2, it is important that PR and earned media channels are reflected here and media considerations or even target media lists should be defined at this juncture.

- *Ecosystem* – Coming out of the audience insights, it is time to start to make some prioritisation when it comes to the channels that are going to be most effective for the task at hand. A campaign ecosystem should be just that – a (usually) visualisation of where the focus should be. I find it useful at this stage to begin to show the relative power and importance of each channel and the nature of the activity – we will come later to talk about paid, earned and owned and the innate challenges with this framework, but it might be useful to identify in the ecosystem where each of these aspects plays a role.

- *Customer journey* – The final planning stage is to create a customer journey. There are many challenges with the construction of a customer journey and wide-ranging industry debate about the benefits (or unnecessary complexity) they bring. However, I still feel it is fundamental, at a macro level, to think about the buying (or conversion) cycle that we would want a customer to go through. The law of averages plays a role here and it is fundamental to remember that audiences do not behave in a rational, neat way. However, as a guiding principle, it is still useful. The customer journey takes the ecosystem and starts to bring some order to it – seeing where content should live and the job it should do. It also links the ecosystem more closely to the behavioural insights from the audience analysis and links both of these back to the campaign objectives.

It is important again to stress that the role of the PR practitioner might not be to construct these; especially, in broader marketing campaigns. However, it is also important to stress the importance of going through this process, even for campaigns or activities that are only PR focussed. For example, there is no reason why a corporate reputation strategy should not go through the above steps – they are all perfectly intuitive for this kind of work and will lead to a better strategic outcome.

Again, the downfall of PR has often been that, because traditional PR equals media relations, the above process is seen as unnecessary as the answer will always just be media relations and the objective will always just be coverage. Digital has thrown these assumptions wide open and mandates the level of analysis outlined earlier to happen if we are truly going to identify the best way to reach and influence our audiences and reach the outcomes the business or organisation requires.

BUILDING A DIGITAL PR STRATEGY

Once these planning tools have been put in place, it is time to construct a strategy. Thus, in a multi-disciplinary setting, there should be one strategy across the board.

A strategy should be the answer to this simple question: using these channels, how do we use marketing communications to reach this audience to achieve this objective?

The question is simple and the information should already have been gathered. The answer in an ideal world should be simple, too. The best strategic thoughts I have worked with are a sentence or two long. They crystallise the mission that everyone is on and clarify the way in which the objective will be achieved. Of course, the approach to define a strategy is not straightforward. Neither is it the sole purpose of this book. In addition, there are so many other fantastically detailed discussions on how to develop a strategy that I will not dwell on it too much here.

Far more relevant, however, are the channel considerations that start to come to the fore. It is necessary to balance the needs of individual channels with an integrated approach that still sits well within the ecosystem and customer journey.

DRAWING THE LINES OF BATTLE AND DEFINING THE ROLE OF PR

It is here, again, where ownership discussions are likely to occur. Although these debates have always been a part and parcel of marketing structures and processes, digital has changed the game. As we have seen, trying to demark what is and is not digital is a fruitless exercise. Digital and social weaves through everything. Paid, earned and owned are not even useful guides as effective earned frequently relies on paid support and paid activities are more successful with earned-worthy content.

The only solution to this conundrum is clarity and collaboration:

- *Clarity* – This comes from senior members of the marketing team being clear about roles and responsibilities. Who is doing what and who oversees different aspects? Even within just a comms team, this is important. It becomes even more vital when the whole marcomms mix is needed. Moreover, this is not just an agency versus agency dynamic. Frequently, the in-house battles are just as fierce. There are many models here that can be used to good effect; for example, the RACI model (which stands for Responsible, Accountable, Consulted and Informed). However, it is important that this does not become a box-ticking exercise. Frequently, I have seen structural plans that look impressively detailed on paper but, frankly, never are glimpsed again once the activity is underway.

- *Collaboration* – In some ways, bringing clarity should be relatively straightforward. That is, when you compare it to embracing a spirit of collaboration. There are many aspects that get in the way of collaboration – profit and loss structures (P&L)s, conflicting objectives (as seen earlier), land-grabs and personal ambition. True collaboration becomes harder the more players are involved. The project lead can play a pivotal role in creating an atmosphere of trust and respect. However, there are practical considerations, too. Regular status updates are one example. (The regularity should be determined by aspects of the project – I've seen everything from daily scrums to bi-weekly catch ups work effectively.) Consistent, integrated reporting and tracking is another. Collaboration in a digital age does not only cover the personnel on the project, but also elements of the campaign; for example, the sharing of content assets and access to data. Workflows that systemise these aspects are crucial.

Making a digital PR ecosystem requires all of the aspects stated earlier. However, this is not just something that can be taught theoretically. It needs to be experienced and practiced. We will look more at internal and agency structures in a later chapter, but this all plays a crucial role in shaping the ecosystem and its effectiveness.

THE ROLE OF CONTENT AND CREATIVE

If the ecosystem is the pipes, then content is usually the water. However, in a complex ecosystem, content can be an inefficient and complex beast to manage. The ecosystem and customer journey should form the basis of a content strategy. What needs to be communicated to each audience at each point? The channels then govern the way content is briefed and produced.

With multiple channels involved, a modular approach to content is important. Take a simple example. One story is to be created within a campaign that will be the heart of a piece of editorial coverage but will also be used as part of a targeted social media campaign and shared with employees via Facebook Workplace. The story is the same, elements of the piece of content will be the same, but the way the content is produced will be different. The video that will be sent to the media will be a different edit to that posted on Facebook and different again to the version – with an introduction from the CEO – that will be shared on Workplace.

The right content built for the right channel is never easy in a multi-channel ecosystem, but is critical to get right.

In addition, this complexity is not going anywhere. Every new technological enhancement brings new ways to treat content. We have been through text, image, video and the next five years will bring virtual reality (VR), augmented reality (AR) and (a new form of) voice.

DIGITAL DISRUPTION WITHIN CHANNELS

So far, we have looked at the role that digital plays at a macro level when it comes to constructing a communication ecosystem and digital PR's role within that. However, there are specific nuances within channels, too. Some of this will be discussed in future chapters 4 and 5 when we look at media relations and social among others in more detail, but it is also worth touching on here.

Take the media as an example. A media strategist now needs to juggle additional complexity when it comes to planning a distribution strategy within this channel. For example, if you get national coverage, this goes online in the early hours of the morning – something that is critical to know if you have global audiences that might be conversing and sharing on social channels. There are certain publications now where their social media footprint is so fundamental that, if you get coverage on their website without it also being seeded out to their social accounts, you have basically negated the impact of that article and the reach is significantly less.

CROSS-CHANNEL IMPACT

Another key argument against siloed thinking in a digital age is the power of cross-channel consumption. At a time when it is easier to share information, we need to unders... channels work together to build influence and impact.

This is another reason why earned, paid, shared and owned are not useful badges to use as the complexity of how information travels merely increases. We will look at more of this in a later chapter 9.

Second screening is a great example of this. Now, a well-built TV advert can lead to social conversation and even direct purchase. A piece of national media coverage can be backed up by targeted Pay Per Click (PPC) search activity to maximise interest in the topic or product. Social retargeting can assist in encouraging people that have shown interest in a particular social post to find out more and move down the funnel.

This is a pivotal part of any ecosystem and customer journey, and one that often is hard to predict. That is why, despite the best planning and strategy, any digital PR campaign needs to have flexibility and agility built in. This not only starts with effective monitoring and listening, but also needs adaptiveness in the way the channel plan has been constructed. If something suddenly takes off, then it is important that resources can be easily redistributed to support and capitalise.

CAMPAIGN CADENCE

The final component of building a digital PR ecosystem is to think about campaign cadence. I use the term 'campaign' loosely here. It could be a long six-month piece of activity or a quick press announcement – but the thinking still applies.

Now, we are clear on what the mix of channels should be, and we are clear that each channel impacts each other. Therefore, we need to find a way to build a campaign executional plan that has the right cadence. This includes our modular approach to content mentioned earlier.

Therefore, if the press embargo lifts on a certain day and time, then when do we expect the coverage to hit and in which publications? When should the social content go live? When does targeted influencer activity start? What is the plan for retargeting? How does the above the line activity play into this? When does the website need to be updated?

In such a multi-channel digital world, none of this can now be left to chance. I have lost count of the number of times I have seen brilliant PR campaigns launch in the national newspapers in the morning, only to visit the brand's social accounts or websites to find absolutely nothing about the announcement. It is this lack of coordination that is primarily the fault of marketing silos. Consumers do not see 'channels' – they just see your brand. If they see something on one channel, they expect it to be mirrored elsewhere.

Customer services have a role to play here too. For making sure that they are armed with the information, they need to be able to respond to incoming enquiries that might be different or unusual because of the PR activity happening that day.

Building an effective campaign cadence is all about ensuring that everything is joined up and that everyone knows her role in the execution.

In this day and age, channel supremacy has gone. Anyone can come into the conversation at any point – and frequently, this will be via mobile devices. Therefore, it is pivotal for us as PR practitioners to think about how all the channels at our disposal (and even the ones we do not control) work together. How should we effectively coordinate them? I have no doubt that anyone working in or with larger consumer businesses will be familiar with the 'TV-first' mentality that exists within traditional marketing functions. This 'matching luggage' approach is dying. It is outdated and only ever creates compromised work in digital channels. We need to find a way to shift this thinking and I believe PR has a big role to play.

MAKING A CASE FOR PR'S SEAT AT THE TABLE

We have already touched on channel 'ownership' and it feels that the PR industry often has a bit of an inferiority complex when it comes to the role of PR in the marketing mix. There are lots of historical – many of them valid – reasons for this. However, in a digital world, there is definitely a growing suggestion that PR's moment has come.

Channel disruption is everywhere across the marketing spectrum. Consumption of linear TV is hitting rock bottom. Consumption of video content has switched to digital and social platforms. Effectiveness of digital display is even lower than in the past, if that were possible.

The one theme all these have in common is attention deficit. With so much information out there, it is harder than ever to get cut through. In addition, interruptive marketing will never win in this environment. Why would I pay attention to a banner ad when the purpose of my visit to a webpage (that I have selectively decided to visit) is going to be what sits between the two skyscrapers at the edge of the page. Consumers are speaking with their actions and clicks.

We stand at a crossroad here. Although consumer behaviours are clear, the formats and technologies have not yet responded. Advertising formats are still stuck in cycle where they are simply replicating what existed in a non-digital world. This approach will fail. However, it will take time.

Content is the answer. However, it is not the content that marketers have used over the last 70 years. Interruptive formats meant we could pick and choose what was presented to an audience. In a world where a consumer of information can pick and choose, we have to work harder. Although this is primarily a discussion around the creation of content, it finds its way back to discussions around channel ownership and ecosystems when you consider that the world of PR is more experienced when it comes to earning attention through content.

Unless you've been on the frontline of a media sell-in and have had the phone slammed down by a journalist who felt your story was not worth of his time (as happened to me on day one of my career as a PR senior account executive), you will not know what it takes to really craft a story that legitimately deserves to have that descriptor.

Telling stories in digital is, of course, a new skill. And one that we will discuss in chapter 6. However, if now is not the time for the PR industry to drop the inferiority complex, then I don't know when is.

QUESTIONS

1. Are you clear on your business objectives and ideal outcomes?

2. Can you build a full campaign ecosystem taking all necessary channels into account?

3. Does everyone in the team understand their role and where the lines are drawn?

4. Do you have one clear strategy across the board that everyone is bought into?

5. Are you clear on how different channels work together to achieve the same goal?

6. What will be your plan to ensure that the cadence of a campaign is effective?

4

MEDIA RELATIONS

There are arguably few industries that have been shaken up by digitisation quite as much as the media industry. Almost every aspect of a publisher's existence has been upturned. From business models and employee skill sets to physical products and distribution – it is a different world than it used to be and digital has been the big shift. Some of the old guard have reacted better than others. And, of course, wherever disruption reigns, there is an opportunity for new entrants.

The digital native publishers are an increasingly powerful force; the likes of Buzzfeed are claiming news scoops that were, in the past, only in reach of the big news brands. The approach and success of these new players – data-first and digital-only – have driven the industry forward and we now sit at a place where many of the traditional publications that have survived are starting to find new, profitable avenues. In addition, at the same time, some of the new upstarts are starting to show signs that they are suffering with the pace of expansion and the cold, hard realities of this resource-intensive industry.

THE EVOLVING MEDIA BUBBLE

It is against this backdrop that we consider media relations. Always a backbone of the PR industry, media relations often, in many ways, feels neglected with the shiny prospects of digital opportunity getting all the focus, investment and glory.

The shifts in the media industry have caused significant impact for those spending time building relationships with the media. Hard-pressed journalists – fewer of them and with more to do with 24-hour news cycles and reams of digital copy to post – are less and less inclined to invest in the PR relationship.

Moreover, it is here that we must also nod to one of the inconvenient truths about the PR industry and media relations in particular – and that is the reality that many journalists see the PR relationship as a necessary evil. More often than not, the reason for this negativity is due to bad practices that are commonplace. Stories are being pitched that have no relevance, or interest, to the journalist in question. The telephone, but especially the rise of email, have been key culprits. Everyone working in the PR industry will have witnessed the 'spray and pray' approach that is so tempting when a 'difficult' story is just failing to get traction.

This quantity over quality approach is often rewarded at a superficial level through digital channels. With more and more 'clickbait' websites out there, getting 'coverage' – even if just a copy and paste rehash of a press release – is certainly possible and at least provides something to add to the daily coverage report. However, we would all be kidding ourselves if we felt this was something that should be seen as in any way valuable to a business or organisation. Even miniscule search engine optimisation (SEO) gains are highly unlikely these days with the added sophistication of Google's search algorithms.

With all the change that is occurring, it is easy to see media relations in a digital age as something of less importance or value. But, that is simply not true. It is just that the approach in a digital age needs to be refined.

CHANGING JOURNALIST PRIORITIES

The first step in this refinement requires a clear understanding of how day-to-day life has changed for the average journalist. The move from regular print deadlines, with clear intervals and demands, has been significant. Add to that the dwindling resources at nearly every major (and minor) publication and you have a perfect storm situation. But, it gets worse. Not only does a shift to digital require more content and more speed in creating it, but it also brings added pressures. Sub-editors are at a premium so prepping an article for publication takes more time. There is a big focus now on journalists being social media brands in their own right, so there is a need to now manage these digital profiles as part of the day job. Moreover, from a pure content standpoint, it is no longer about copy and a hero image. The trend is towards new, multimedia and interactive storytelling to get cut through.

Does it sound familiar? So much of this mirrors the challenges that are faced in the PR industry too. But, this also helps to give an insight into the environment through which media relations activities find themselves.

THE NEW 'JOURNALISTS'

So, this is the environment for an average journalist. In addition, this professional moniker is important. The formalised relationship between PR and journalist brings certain unspoken assumptions – things like conventions around embargos or 'off the record' and the structural considerations of a press release. Of course, any good practitioner will tell you there's no such thing as a watertight embargo or being 'off the record', but the conventions are there and understood by all involved, even if they are contravened.

In a digital world where anyone can publish anything at any moment, it is not just traditional, professional journalists that the average PR will come up against.

Bloggers were the first new kids on the block. Suddenly, technology provided an opportunity for citizen journalists and commentators to have a mouthpiece that could potentially reach large audiences. While they rarely deal in hard news, they are a source of information and insight, especially in more niche circles. But, the average blogger, unlike the average journalist, has none of the professional training and knows nothing of the PR conventions that exist elsewhere.

Suddenly, the picture becomes far more complex and the traditional PR approach likely to be far less effective.

Social influencers bring further challenges and, although we will cover the topic of influencer marketing in a lot more depth in chapter 7, much of what follows still applies.

A DATA-LED APPROACH TO MEDIA LISTS

When considering this new environment, as mentioned in Chapter 2, data should sit at the heart of any approach to digital PR. Moreover, when it comes to media relations, the data needs to inform one of the most important tools of the trade – the media list. The media list is the modern equivalent of the little black book. But, rather than being a personal tool filled with relationship-based insight, media lists are symptomatic scale and efficiency; large excel documents that many will be familiar with, including contact details for journalists, organised into sectoral segments.

Technology has made this even easier. Many database tools now exist to keep this information up to date and provide lists literally at the click of a button.

But, media lists and their ease of creation have produced some of the most challenging issues to face our industry and have jeopardised, more than anything else, the relationship between journalist and PR. It is no surprise that, when faced with a list of email addresses for journalists that are, at a superficial level, potentially interested in a certain story, topic or theme, there is an innate attraction to simply mail merge the press release to the entire database and see what sticks.

Despite efforts by some journalists over the years to name and shame, there is actually no real penalty for this type of approach. And, it flies in the wind of every piece of best practice advice around media relations: know your contact and craft a pitch that is suited to them. This takes far more work than just hunting down an email address and actually requires research into what the journalist covers and knowledge of how they best like to be contacted.

KILLING THE PRESS RELEASE

The press release is another culprit in this drama. Or, rather, it is another tool that has been corrupted. The traditional press release has a lot going for it. For example, clear, succinct presentation of information that can be easily navigated by a journalist and used in a piecemeal way to pull together a story quickly and easily. And yet, most press releases have become great volumes with too much content and so couched in marketing-speak that trying to uncover the 'story' hidden within (if it is even present) is like swimming through treacle.

The Social Media News Release (SMNR) was at one point seen as the great saviour. And, in truth it too had a lot going for it. The idea was simple – a digital version of the press release that cut things up into bite-sized chunks so that a journalist could access everything she needed in one place – copy, links, images, social media accounts, etc. I have also seen many elaborate systems that include email-marketing-like approaches where you can track who opened the email, which link they clicked on and even offered journalists the ability to chat with the PR – all through the SMNR system. Again, there is a lot to like with these approaches. However, fundamentally it always felt a bit like trying to revive a process that has broken for other reasons.

Because the way the information is presented is only half of the problem. It is often the information itself that is lacking and the way it is (or is not) then crafted for the specific individual.

Of course, the press release is not going anywhere. Until journalists stop asking for PRs to 'send me the press release', press releases will never die. But as digital PR continues to become the norm, as journalists continue to suffer more and more time pressures and as we see more non-professional players come into the ecosystem, we need to be constantly thinking about the way we best present information to our intended audience.

The SMNR was something that offered a possible solution and for a few years gathered a degree of interest. The idea behind it was sound – provide all the elements of a story that a journalist needed, online, and allow them to pick and choose to create a story. Hosting it online saved email traffic and opened up opportunities to provide other multimedia content quickly and easily.

However, the SMNR did not really solve most of the problems that blighted the traditional press release (apart from perhaps the emphasis on facts and information rather than 'PR padding' but this is just as possible through a SMNR – it just depends on the person using it!) And, that is because it is still essentially providing the same information to everyone, whereas the opportunity with digital PR, and the role of media relations within this, is to provide targeted stories and approaches to specific journalists that engage them directly. And, that is absolutely possible with digital PR.

It is also worth acknowledging the role – and importance for many businesses – of some sort of press centre. This should not be a turgid list of the latest press releases but should include useful information that a journalist can use when writing a story. It should have galleries of images, video (with option to download in a range of formats, including high definition), biographies on spokespeople, links to annual reports and other important documents and background information on the company. This should be easily accessible on the corporate website and clearly signposted. It remains a valuable tool for the media to use.

Too often, the press release becomes a lazy way to demonstrate success. If we issue a release every day – as some companies do (and some do more) – then no one can ever accuse us of not generating news. And yet, they are not news, they are noise. So, ask yourself the tough questions: is this content interesting? And if it is, is a press release really the most engaging way to convey it? The answer to both questions will often be 'no'.

Obviously, I am painting a worst-case scenario of the state of media relations. There are many brilliant practitioners out there that follow best practice. But, it remains in many places a discipline that is pushed to the lowest level employee who is overworked and has been given very limited training on the so-called 'best practice' approaches.

Digital offers a way to reinvent media relations in order to overcome some of the challenges that have blighted the discipline and ensure effectiveness.

TOWARDS A NEW MEDIA STRATEGY

We have looked at the pressure on journalists and, in chapter 1, we have also looked at the changing media ecosystem. There, we saw that a focus on data is key. Understanding the audience you are looking to reach, and their media consumption habits, is the first step. It might be that, for certain audiences, your media list of hundreds of publications will be meaningless. There might only be a handful of publications – or sometimes even just one or two – that will be successful in reaching the people you want to reach.

This gives you the freedom to really think about crafting a story and an approach that will pique their interest and engage them effectively.

It is also worth understanding the channels by which this audience will engage with media content. For example, if you are targeting an audience that only ever consumes news on social channels (and that number is growing significantly), then this needs to be a key part of your strategy. Not every story that is published by the media ends up on their social feeds, even though this is where many of them are now getting significant reach and traction. So, if your coverage only appears on the website – or even in print – it might be totally ineffective for the target audience because it is not reaching them where they are.

This level of understanding also feeds into the content you need to support the sell-in. Increasingly, publishers are looking towards new forms of articles.

BBC News Labs (2017) on Medium has published a fascinating look at some of the new formats being embraced by media publishers and journalists. Here is a flavour of some of them:

- *Short and vertical video* – often with captions, pioneered by publications like AJ+ and NowThis.

- *Horizontal stories* – swipeable cards like Snapchat Stories and its clones.

- *Longform scrollytelling* – evolved from the original *New York Times* Snowfall.

- *Structured news* – like the original Circa or the reusable cards at Vox.com.

- *Live blogs* – frequently used for big events.

- *Listicles* – like Buzzfeed.

- *Newsletters and briefings* – which seem to be on trend right now.

- *Timelines* – which I expected to be more common.

- *Bots and chat* – from the chat-styled Qz app to the many attempts to deliver news within chat apps.

- *Personalised* – which typically is used to filter the choice of stories, rather than the story itself.

- *Data visualisation* – from graphs to interactives.

- *VR and AR* – pioneered by publishers like the *New York Times*.

These are the types of formats that are now being embraced and, in some cases, prioritised by editors – they are getting prime positions and being syndicated across channels. So,

ـg ways to provide content that can fit into these new formats will be a key way of ensuring that resulting coverage succeeds.

THE SELL-IN

Once you are clear on the audience, the right media targets and the sort of article that might be seen as a good outcome for the audience target, it is necessary to start thinking about the digital media approach.

Here, it is still useful to tier media – as per the above discussion, there will be some that the data show are more effective for your audience. For major announcements or stories, it is worth contacting these publications in advance. Traditionally, especially for the larger publications, it would be worth approaching the relevant editor or news desk to find the journalist that will be most receptive to the news. In a digital era, this still might be the best option, but it is worth considering other avenues.

At a time when formats such as video – as seen earlier – are often given prominence, it is useful to think about other targets within the editorial team that might be worth speaking to – for example, the video editor or interactive team. This gives you an opportunity to co-create a story and provide the assets needed. A data editor is often a great person to speak with if you have a story that has a large data component, especially if raw data is available for their teams to analyse.

Social media also offers new opportunities when it comes to outreach to individual journalists. As we have seen already, email overload is a problem for journalists and finding a way to stand out gives you more chance of success. So, it is worth considering other channels. Twitter, in particular, is a channel that the media have embraced in a big way – mainly because it is an asynchronous network – meaning that most profiles are visible even if you do not follow each other. This gives the media a great opportunity to build a new distribution channel and a way to use the network to spot news and track sources.

There is clearly no point in recreating the 'spray-and-pray' approach outlined earlier. Bad practices will fail no matter what the channel. But, if you have a good relationship with a journalist and you feel you have a story that is relevant and interesting, contacting them via a social network can be a great way to engage in a less formal way and discuss the pros and cons of any particular story or opportunity.

GOING BACK TO BASICS

Of course, a lot of the more traditional media relations approaches and techniques still apply. Digital has not changed the game entirely, but, at a time when the media themselves will be increasingly thinking about how stories can work on digital and social channels, understanding this need and priority when engaging with them can ensure that the right content is being provided to them in the right way at the right time.

In addition, it will vary from case to case. Some media might still be attracted by the conventions of the past – press releases, interviews and press trips. Others will merely be put off by this approach. Ultimately, the quality of the story itself will always hold the most sway. However, the way it is sold can have a pretty big impact on the quality of the resulting coverage.

It is worth mentioning here that Twitter and other networks can also be a great tool for identification. Not just tracking down the right journalist – as most traditional media databases should still win out here. But instead finding out a bit more about your target – what they are interested in, what they have covered recently and even interests outside their professional capacity which could come in useful. By being involved in relevant discussion – in an authentic way – you can also often strike up great relationships and really immerse yourself in a topic, finding out interesting potential story angles and uncovering new sources of influence that you can then build into future media plans and strategies. Social listening tools offer many opportunities to scale this approach, by setting up searches and alerts for specific topics or among particular groups of people.

Some journalists have now started 'breaking news' on their social accounts before they have even published a story. This is another interesting opportunity, especially if the journalist has a large following. Allowing them to break an embargo through social media could be a key driver in igniting a conversation if that is the ambition of a particular campaign or approach. It is also an area to be cautious around if the timing of an announcement is key.

MEDIA PARTNERSHIPS

As new digital publishers come into the mix – the likes of Buzzfeed and UNILAD – the growth of commercial opportunities within the media environment has been fast and, in many cases, pretty innovative.

Of course, the relationship between editorial and commercial is nothing new in the media environment. But, the boundaries have started to blur. Coming via the traditional approach of the advertorial, publishers have realised that their new content creation skill sets – especially, those that are rooted in digital and social – are of interest to brands. Buzzfeed has invested significantly in talent and facilities to create social-first content that is unequalled.

We risk entering into all sorts of ethical and philosophical debates when we consider the role of paid media in media outreach. And, we will come onto talk about some of this in more detail later. But, the reality is that entering into a commercial relationship with publishers and co-creating with them can result in pretty significant outputs and outcomes. Match this to the fact that you can then use paid media targeting to help this content reach a specific audience and you have a powerful new tool.

This is something that is still relatively unregulated. Disclosing the nature of the relationship is important but the degree to which this is done transparently massively varies. In the past, the differentiation between advertorial and editorial was clear. It is much less so online, especially through social. The major publishers are still consistent in their approach but the new age publishers and influencers are far less so. It is a challenge for the industry but that should not detract from what can be a very attractive opportunity for businesses and organisations.

Native advertising has promised much but has taken a long time to mature. We are now getting to a stage where the content opportunities are such that this is an avenue and area that is definitely worth considering as part of your media strategy, audience dependent.

SYNDICATION

While we are looking at issues around paid media, another area – which again will be discussed further in due course – is the role of syndication, both organic and paid.

It is a pretty simple principle. If you receive great coverage, then that will reach the organic audience of that publication. But, it is important not to overlook the fact that this coverage could be powerful for other audiences too. Again, this is not necessarily anything new – media coverage has often been used in other contexts to show credibility and third party validation. But, digital offers new opportunities to do this at scale.

At a very basic level, sharing coverage on owned channels supported by paid media to reach new targets is an effective way to build and develop reputation. You control the targeting so you can ensure it reaches the very people you want to influence.

But, there are other avenues to explore here too. Content syndication networks have sprung up and offer effective ways to natively reach new audiences, using existing third-party content. This could be within the websites of publications themselves – for example, commonly through the 'if you like this, then you might like this' sections that you will usually see at the foot of articles. Or, increasingly, this is possible through native placements in feeds on publisher (or other) websites. The placement will be marked as an advert but, as long as the title has been effectively constructed (and most of these platforms give you the opportunity to split test different lines), these can be highly effective ways to get your message out to a new audience.

THE DIGITAL SPOKESPERSON

We will touch on building thought leadership in the corporate chapter 10 but it is worth touching here on the use of spokespeople in the digital space. Digital – and social media in particular – does not just offer journalists the opportunity to build a following directly – it offers the same to corporate or brand leaders. Where it was once necessary to convey thoughts or business shifts through the media, these days it is possible to do it direct. There are positives and negatives to this approach. The positives are that, at best, it brings increased authenticity and transparency – you feel as though you are hearing from that CEO directly. However, there is a danger that, if done in the wrong way, it feels like propaganda. The third-party validation that a media report or story brings can sometimes be invaluable – to bring rigour and validity to an announcement or argument. But, there are times when the personal approach works well. And, we will discuss some of this more when we come to look at crisis communications in the digital realm.

At the heart of making this strategy a success – as we will also see when it comes to crisis management – is building a profile for the senior stakeholder that feels true and genuine. They need to be invested in the process and be open to using digital channels to communicate with an external audience. If the account is merely used as a way to distribute corporate messaging, then it will serve a purpose but will not be massively effective as a story generating (or reputation protecting) vehicle.

However, if the stakeholder in question is fully invested, then it is possible to build high profile communities around them and use such an account as a powerful way to attract and manage media interest.

However, be warned, there have been many cringeworthy examples of where members of a company's C-suite have used social media in a way that certainly should not have been advised. It is a fine line, but one that could be worth risking for the rewards that it will potentially bring.

BROADCAST, VIDEO AND LIVE CONTENT

This brings us nicely onto the area of video and live content. Video – as we have noted already – is fast becoming a favourite format for media publications – beyond the broadcast media where it has obviously always been key. Being able to offer high quality – and authentic – video content to support an announcement or story will pay dividends, and is likely to make the resulting coverage more engaging, but will hopefully also enhance the placement of the story, as has been discussed.

Over the last few years, live video content has been something that the social networks have rushed to embrace – Facebook in particular and, at time of writing, the Facebook algorithm is significantly prioritising live video content. So, that is one potential reason to use it.

But, live video comes with a whole host of challenges and I generally find myself advising people not to use it rather than encouraging them to do so. The bottom line is that there are actually very few examples – at least for a brand – where live content makes sense. Live is about a moment in time – but it has to be a pretty compelling moment in time for someone to want to tune in and see content live.

Very few businesses have these situations on a regular basis. That has not to say you cannot share video of an event or situation. However, by not streaming it live, you give yourself the time and space to create an edit that is likely to be far slicker and documents the event more effectively. This also gives you the advantage of getting the content reviewed and approved before it hits the digital airwaves. So, for me, the dangers of live often outweigh the opportunities.

PROVIDING ACCESS TO EVENTS THROUGH DIGITAL

Another area where PR and media relations is often brought into play is through events. Events – such as press conferences, trade/corporate conferences and trade shows – offer opportunities to hold a journalist's attention or give them a deeper delve into something you are hoping to promote. They also offer a fruitful opportunity to connect in person, which is increasingly rare these days.

Many of the traditional best practices, when it comes to events like this, definitely apply. But, there are a few that should be considered in the digital age. For example, very simple ones like providing good access to WiFi! Also, approaches that are more nuanced. It is amazing how many events still fail to create and/or promote a specific hashtag. If you have people that are following remotely and want to be able to find relevant content, then this is the key, and for journalists – both those attending and those not able to. Press packs are another area that need to be wholly rethought – and, usually access to some online repository is the best approach – providing multimedia and image-based content, of course. Finally, it is often worth thinking about whether it is possible and/or financially beneficial to provide studio facilities on-site to enable the media to conduct interviews and/or create – or co-create – content for dissemination, either live or after the event.

QUESTIONS

1. How does the changing media ecosystem affect the approach you take to media relations?

2. How do you need to approach journalist outreach given their changing time pressures?

3. How do bloggers and influencers fit with your more traditional journalist contacts?

4. What changes need to be made to the way you build a media list?

5. Is it time to take a cold hard look at whether your approach to press releases is working?

6. Do you issue too many press releases? Is this information interesting? Can it be presented in a different way?

7. Does your content match the format that journalists are now using to craft stories?

8. What is the best way to reach your journalist target?

9. Should you look into investing in partnerships with key media?

10. How can you syndicate media content beyond the initial audience?

5

SOCIAL MEDIA

There is no doubt that social media is the biggest shift that has ever happened to the PR industry. Its rise has been meteoric and it has forced businesses and organisations to entirely rethink the way they communicate and engage with their audiences. It is also something that has transformed the news media and required the latter to rethink everything they do from storytelling to distribution. It is hard to overestimate the impact that social media has had and, therefore, it is something that will be sprinkled throughout this book. But, given its significance, it absolutely warrants its own, focused analysis and a thorough look at the impact it has had.

It is easy to forget – with this backdrop – that social media is relatively young. MySpace was only founded in 2003; Facebook in 2004. Even if you factor in forums and blogging, it is hard to argue that social media – at least in a way that reaches mass audiences – is more than 20 years old. And, as with any immature discipline, the road that it has been on during that time has been rocky and treacherous. At the time of writing, social media is being blamed (and not for the first time) – by some – for altering the course of democratic elections, sharing user data without permission and having significant influence on the population at large that is still largely unregulated.

This, alongside technological developments and changes in consumer behaviour, has required social networks to evolve and develop to a place where they look very different to what existed 5 years ago, let alone 10 or 20.

THE SOCIAL MEDIA JOURNEY FOR BRANDS

This journey for businesses and organisations has been equally varied. I still remember the early days of social media marketing where social media was viewed with scepticism and any suggestion that this should be something that warranted significant attention and/or budget was unlikely to be supported. That all changed when social started to grow in prominence. When the likes of Twitter and Facebook started hitting the front pages of the *Financial Times* and other newspapers, senior stakeholders started to take note and things changed very quickly. This is what I like to think of as the social gold rush. Accounts (often multiple ones) were set up on all the available networks and money and resources were pumped into updating these channels with content. This was in the good old days of organic reach and community building was seen as a key objective.

The overriding sense at this point was that social media was going to be big and that 'we just need to be there'. This was often prompted by the unstrategic fact that competitors were doing it. At the time, there was a lot of talk about how social allowed for one-to-one dialogue with customers and audiences, but there was less discussion about whether this was a good thing and, more crucially, whether it could ever scale. Unfortunately, this whole period left businesses in a state of social stasis, where they had amassed these large operations that were resource intensive (despite the fact that social at this stage was 'free', it still required significant internal and external resource).

WHEN SOCIAL GOT STRATEGIC

Then, the big shift happened. The main networks were experiencing massive user growth and, inevitably, the question of monetisation was becoming louder and louder. In 2007, Facebook founder and chief executive officer, Mark Zuckerberg, announced the launch of Facebook Ads:

> *Facebook Ads represent a completely new way of advertising online. For the last hundred years media has been pushed out to people, but now marketers are going to be a part of the conversation. And they're going to do this by using the social graph in the same way our users do. (Facebook Newsroom, 2007).*

The birth of ads was followed by a series of algorithm changes that started to reduce the organic reach of Facebook Pages (as opposed to personal ones) to the point where, at time of writing, the potential organic reach of most brand pages hovers just above zero. The commercial effect of this for Facebook is clear. The challenge for brands has been massive.

And, brands have often been slow to adapt. I see many brand pages that are still obviously posting organically and only getting a handful of engagements with their content – and many of these are probably the marketing team themselves. You have to look at something like this and question the point in even undertaking social activities for this level of return. The slow adoption is easy to understand. When you have had something for free, making the case that you now need to pay is hard. And, there is a lot of bad feeling as a result.

Of course, Facebook is not the only network that has gone down this path – almost every other network has brought algorithmic feeds into play, but Facebook has the upper hand by splitting out personal and business (or non-personal) accounts.

The reality is that this shift has required businesses to totally rethink their approach to Facebook. It is now not about your followers, it is about the audience you really want to reach (of which your followers may or may not be a part). It is actually, with hindsight, the right move for brands – the targeting (as we have already looked at) available on Facebook almost makes paying for reach worthwhile, but it still requires a significant rethink of approach.

Social media moves an incredible pace. One week, I counted 12 major new feature announcements by the main social networks. And, that is not totally unusual. This pace is hard to stay on top of. With all of the above taken into consideration, despite social media's relative youthfulness as a discipline, I feel as though we have reached a period of social maturity. Where the technology and potential approaches are such that social media can be seen – done in the right way – as a business critical channel that offers significant contribution to a company's bottom line. And, I can think of very few businesses where this will nor be the case.

WHO OWNS SOCIAL?

There is no doubt that social media has become a part of the fabric of our lives. This brings a number of challenges for the marketer. But, principally there is the issue of ownership. There are many parts of a business that are now touched by social. Marketing is the obvious one but it can also stretch to

HR, product development and, of course, customer service. Any community manager will also be familiar with the old refrain of 'can you just pop this up on Twitter'. A marketing director once told me that social media was where they put all their announcements that 'weren't good enough to be press releases'. And, look at many corporate accounts – especially on Twitter – and you do get a sense that the account has become a dumping ground for content.

The answer to the original question is that no one owns social and neither should they. But, I think we will shift from a place where a marketing team is the default social owner to one where you have a social gatekeeper team that become the guardians of the feeds. They are tasked with understanding the reasons for why the business is using social; for upholding elements like consistent tone of voice and visual identity and ensuring that a quality control filter is applied. They are also likely to be the people that manage the use of paid media either directly, or through an agency.

But it is not just reactive, these people should be staying on top of the myriad of changes that happen to social technologies and being the ones that advise and encourage the business to explore new avenues. For example, working with the customer services team to develop chatbot functionality. They are social innovators and their reach is far beyond just the marketing department. In fact, they should work closely with marketing and communications (internal and external) to ensure that everything is planned and ready in advance.

DEVELOPING A SOCIAL STRATEGY

One of the main aspects this team needs to create and then uphold is the social strategy. At the heart of a good social strategy is an understanding of a business's 'social purpose'.

What is the role that social is going to play for your business (and there may be more than one). So many brands seem to be confused about what social is actually doing for their business and the bottom line. Social feeds are a mishmash of different types of content, with different messages. Anyone following the content would be confused as to what they have signed up to. Social has so many benefits for a business – from top of funnel awareness to delivering conversion at the other end. So, clarity on how it is to be used is vital.

A social purpose does not just encapsulate content; it stretches from objectives right the way through to measurement and KPIs. It includes visual identity and tone of voice. It is also a great way to get everyone on the same page. Social often lies at the intersection of the whole business – as we have seen – and thus creating a document (often called a Playbook) that summarises the social purpose and all the other strategic priorities of the business is key, not just for the social team, but for disseminating across a business to get a clear understanding of the role of social and what it should – and should not – do.

A core part of this will be channel selection and here we will not dwell too long as much of this has already been covered above and the process is very similar to that discussed. An understanding of the target audience and their media consumption will allow for a clear and informed decision about which social channels are the right ones to select and use. There are some nuances here with social. For far too long, many businesses have treated social media as a homogenous whole. If you visit their different channels on different platforms, then you will see the same content, at best tweaked to fit the channel. This radically overlooks the fact that we all use different channels at different times in different ways. So, working out the role that each channel plays in your social purpose and within your ecosystem is critical. Think about the features and advantages that each channel brings. Think about how your audience will use them and the information they will be looking for as a result.

CONTENT PLANNING

A central part of any social media approach is content planning. In much the same way as PR, social media is a real-time channel. It rewards relevance and timeliness. This does not mean you have to jump on every news moment but it does mean that content distributed through social should feel as though it is speaking to the audience at a time that is appropriate to them and their lives. So, it is important that the content strategy finds that intersection of what is right for the brand and what is right for the audience. This should happen at a macro level (coming from the social purpose) and at a post-by-post level.

Plotting out the content plan is something that exists within a conversation calendar – a pretty standard element within the industry these days. However, there are a number of issues with the traditional conversation calendar approach. First among these is that it often prioritises quantity of content. You see a list of days laid out in front of you and the temptation is to fill them all with content. As we have seen earlier, this is no longer a wise strategy based on everything we know about developments in social media generally. As paid becomes a reality for most channels, less is more is the key. In addition, that means a quality-over-quantity approach comes into play. Much better to have only one post per week but make sure it is the best it can be and has a significant media budget behind it.

This should be a liberating experience for social content teams. Rather than feeling obliged to churn out content that is often subpar, you can really focus on content that is going to make a difference. But, this is a big adjustment for businesses who are used to having conversation calendars filled with content.

The other problem with conversation calendars is that they tend to overlook evergreen content. Because, while social media is a discipline that is often about the here and now, it is important to remember that certain timely moments happen all the time to different people but at different times – and social gives us a way to target them. For example, you are a baby furniture brand and you want to target new mums and dads – you can use social media to identify people that have just had a new arrival and deliver them congratulatory content. That will not fit into a conversation calendar – it is a piece of content that needs to be always-on, waiting for that next moment. I call this cyclical content and it is worth pausing and thinking about whether it could apply to you and your business.

Retargeting is another great example of cyclical content. We will look more at retargeting in the paid media section but this is essentially the way by which you identify people that have shown interest in a product or service – most often by visiting your website – and you then use this information to retarget them with content that helps to move them down the conversion funnel. This is cyclical because it happens all the time, at different times, to different people.

It is also worth touch on the issue of 'matching luggage' – where campaign content on different channels needs to look the same as the core campaign idea – here, as it applies to social media. Many teams working in social will be familiar with the request to put the TV commercial up on Facebook. This plays into the 'social dumping ground' concept identified earlier. It also diminishes the role of social to that of a distribution channel. It also wholly overlooks the way in which people use different social channels. For example, when it comes to video, letterbox dimensions do not perform well – with the trend towards vertical video increasing and providing better engagement. Also, most TV commercials employ a traditional storytelling narrative with the brand often revealing itself towards the end. When you have three seconds to grab someone's attention through video on social, this is often not the best approach.

Of course, there will be plenty of times when social media will need to play a role within a bigger campaign. But, there are also likely to be moments when there is an opportunity for social media to taking a campaign role itself, within the channel. Increasingly, I think it is useful to think of content on social as mini-campaigns rather than standalone posts. It is another area where conversation calendars can help but where they often encourage individual post thinking rather than how they connect. Rather than serving the same content to an audience, think about how you can craft a series of pieces of content that will really stand out over a long period of time, which are linked; possibly, with some retargeting included as well.

CONTENT TYPES AND FORMATS

So far, we have focused quite a bit on traditional posts or posts with image or video content, but social media – spurred by paid media – has started to include a range of different content formats that promise far greater engagement. Here are some of the most interesting content formats that are worth considering.

Image

It is easy to forget how significant an announcement it was when images were finally supported on social channels – particularly on Twitter. It is now pretty rare to see content on social media that is not accompanied by one or more images or video. And, engagement rates have consistently shown that this is a good approach. It is not surprising – you are taking more of the feed real estate with a more arresting piece of content versus just text. Increasingly, there are more and more options when it comes to images, including collages and other gallery-type options.

Video

As technology has developed, the use of video across social channels has become much more of a possibility and, again, the networks – and brands – have embraced video. Mark Zuckerberg came out and said in 2016 (USA Today, 2016) that Facebook was going to be a video-first network. In 2017 in the United States, Facebook launched a dedicated video channel called Facebook Watch, and it was due to launch in the United Kingdom in 2018. Video is going nowhere and, for all the reasons already identified with image content, it is easy to see why. Networks have experimented with a number of ways of displaying video, including autoplay, so it is important to be aware of the specifications for the channel you are focused on. As we have already seen, there are a number of other considerations when it comes to video – for example, with mobile, is it better to have vertical video? As people are scrolling through their feed, your content needs to 'stop their thumb' so having video content that grabs you in the first few seconds is key – and users rarely watch until the end so do not leave the crucial information until then. Many watch video on social media with sound turned off, so that is another consideration, but, on the flipside, with things like Facebook Watch and Snapchat Discover, there is more of a focus on long-form video being something that consumers are embracing through social channels. So, video presents a massive opportunity but there are a lot of different aspects to consider to get it right.

Canvas

Canvas ads are now something that exist across the Facebook ecosystem of apps. Canvas is a fully immersive, website-like experience. It is full screen and allows you creative freedom to develop a vertical scroll experience including elements of your choosing – whether that is image, text, video or buttons and calls to action. Crucially, Canvases load in the background so they are immediately available to the user and do not require people to click into a web browser to find more information.

Stories

Ephemeral content – that disappears after a set period of time – was pioneered by Snapchat through its Stories feature. In the last few years the other networks have copied this feature, and now you can find similar examples on Facebook, Facebook Messenger, WhatsApp and Instagram. Usage of this feature has skyrocketed – often to the detriment of Snapchat. And, brands have started to explore the opportunities, including being able to link through to a website or other online engagement.

Carousels and Collections

It is a form of advertising product where a series of images or videos can be linked together in a scrolling gallery to help tell a story or show different products. Recently on Facebook,

Collections have also become popular as a way of providing more information on products as well as links to buy.

All these formats provide a wealth of opportunity to really engage audiences in new ways. But, there are challenges too. Many of them require more sophisticated production and require creative and content teams to be up to speed on the new offerings, opportunities and how to create them.

The majority of interactions with social channels are now via mobile devices and so it is understandable that the majority of the formats mentioned are optimised for mobile. This has been a big shift for the networks but one that has been totally embraced by them and the user base. As we move from mobile into other mediums including voice, it will be interesting to see how the platforms further develop their offerings and the opportunities for brands.

SOCIAL MEDIA TARGETING

As alluded to earlier, one of the forced outcomes of the shift to pay-to-play with social media is that it opens up powerful ways to target audiences directly. For an industry that has always struggled with anything but broad brush reach, the ability to use native formats but with super-charged targeting is transformational. Campaigns can have new layers of complexity with different messages being targeted at different audiences.

Access to data also characterises the ability to measure on social channels, even though still too much measurement is based around metrics such as engagement or reach, which are indicators of success but are still hard to translate or link through to business goals. We will discuss more about social targeting, data and measurement in the next few chapters 9 and 11.

BUILDING AND SUSTAINING A COMMUNITY

One of the oft-neglected aspects of social media marketing is community management. I actually have an issue with the term community management as it suggests a community is something that can be 'managed', which is not the case. The best community managers I have ever worked with are more like community facilitators. The worst are merely people that post content and copy and paste answers to incoming questions. Community management can transform a brand – just look at examples like Innocent Smoothies or Tesco Mobile, where a well thought-through and activated community management approach can build brand reputation and loyal advocates.

At the heart of good community management lies a clear tone of voice. Personifying a brand is never easy. It is useful to think about some of those old tricks – such as imagining if your brand was a celebrity: who would it be? As we move into a world where voice is going to play more of a role, the tone of voice will reach a point where it is no longer something that is just conveyed in text but actually in an audible way.

Because of this, the process of constructing a tone of voice is an exercise that should involve all parts of a business. Its use is perhaps most visible through social media content but effective tone of voice is something that could extend throughout all the different ways a business communicates – from all types of advertising, to customer service and website copy. Again, your audience only sees your brand – whether consumer or corporate – so having a consistent tone of voice across all platforms and channels is important.

Building a community is also different to the past when your fans and followers were more likely to see your content on a regular basis. Now, the sense of community on social channels – at least in a scalable way – tends to be more fleeting.

You might build up debate and discussion around a particular post, rather than always having the same group of people commenting day-after-day.

There is no doubt that recapturing a sense of community – bringing the social back into social – is something that the networks (and Facebook in particular) are very focused on. Facebook's recent algorithm shifts are prioritising content that truly engages, content that inspires comment and debate rather than just passive consumption. The networks are seeking to ensure that social media stays social. This is a good thing for quality, branded content that grasps your attention and for the practice of community management.

Another important aspect of community management is customer service. This is an area that has grown considerably since the early days of social media. As brands started to expand their social media presence, audiences quickly realised that contacting a brand on social often elicited a quicker response than via traditional customer service channels such as phone or email. Often, there were a number of factors behind this. The quantity of messages on social at that time, compared to other customer service channels (far fewer) would certainly have had an impact, and the fact that social channels were likely be managed by dedicated community managers – often totally divorced from the traditional customer service operation, which meant they were able to assist customers directly as part of their ongoing activities.

As the industry has developed and evolved, this has changed. The quantity of incoming customer service enquiries through social has increased significantly and with it, a need to streamline customer service operations has occurred. Technology has also come to the fore here and rightly so. Businesses need to aim for a situation where they have 'one view' of a customer – across all channels. Again, they only see one brand – they do not see different channels. So, if they contact you via Twitter, they expect you to know about the enquiry they made via telephone two weeks ago. This complexity requires new ways to look at the problem and new, technology- and data-driven solutions.

Underpinning all of this is a question about where community management sits within an organisation. There are a number of different options:

Internal Contact Centre

One solution is to put the entire community management process into the company's internal contact centre. This navigates round the issues with 'one view' and ensures that the people handling customer services enquiries are there to provide the most accurate advice possible. Clearly, proper training will be needed here – especially around tone of voice – and the team will need to be trained and kept up to speed on marketing activities that are going through the channels so they can pick things up that are not just true customer service enquiries. This latter element is where this often falls down.

Internal Hybrid

It is the solution that I often feel presents the best outcome. In this scenario, you have a dedicated community manager team internally that handles all posting and marketing activities (including responding to the community around anything that is not related to customer services) and then you have a dedicated social customer services team – within the contact centre environment – that is dedicated to social media customer service. You then have a technology workflow that allows engagements on social to be triaged and sent to the right team.

External Hybrid

This approach is very similar to the internal hybrid approach, except that the community management team (usually) is outsourced to an agency or third-party supplier. This often works well but I still feel that often the best place for community management to sit is in the heart of the business rather than being outsourced to someone else.

External

And then, there is the solution whereby everything is outsourced to a third party – and there are very good suppliers that can assist with this sort of arrangement. Often, this is required because of headcount and resource challenges internally. However, as for the reasons above, I do not believe it is the best solution, all things being equal.

In certain industries, there are additional challenges when it comes to community management. The most obvious is in regulated industries. For example, the health care industry – in the United Kingdom at least – has specific considerations around adverse event reporting. An adverse event is when a patient discusses ill effects they had during the time they were taking a particular medication. Under Association of the British Pharmaceutical Industry (ABPI) regulations, an adverse event might be reported and investigated immediately as soon as it is discovered. The onus is on the company to monitor social media for adverse events and be proactive in their attempts. This is a significant undertaking for many pharmaceutical brands and a contributing factor to generally slow adoption of digital and social technologies by health-care businesses.

Before we leave community management, it is worth just touching on two final issues.

The first is crisis – which we will discuss again in the later chapter 11 dedicated to this. Crisis situations often occur first on social media these days; so, having dedicated listening and good escalation processes are absolutely vital to be a first warning when something goes wrong.

The second area, which again will be discussed in more detail later, is the role that emerging technologies will have on customer service and community management. For example, chatbots and automation are emerging solutions that could be game changing for this environment. It is likely that a lot of the enquiries that a company receives on a regular basis through social media are all questions that have pretty clear answers that could be automated – providing less of a resource drain on the business and a better experience for customers.

USING SOCIAL FOR CONVERSION

Social media has always promised much when it comes to conversion. Finally, there might be an opportunity to clearly link top of funnel content marketing on social media with some sort of conversion point. Certainly, social media can be an effective traffic driver (although merely asking someone to click on a link in social media to load a website will give you a significant drop off rate). But, social commerce has always struggled. Most of the major social networks have been experimenting with social commerce since about 2014. They have introduced buy buttons and various other advertising units that will aid conversion. But, it has yet to fully be taken up by consumers.

If you visit Asia, you will see the difference immediately. There, apps like WeChat have commerce built in – you can order a taxi, your laundry or even pay for a meal in a restaurant all through WeChat's app. It has a ubiquity – in China at least – that I doubt we will ever see from an app here in the Western world, but it still points to what is possible.

And, consumer behaviour in the United States and Europe is starting to point to this trend gathering pace. Mobile saturation is here already but the technology is starting to catch pace too. Mobile payment is now pretty common on our high streets and paying on a mobile using a fingerprint or even your face is now possible and something that increasing numbers of consumers are adopting.

So, the time feels right for social commerce to finally make an impact. The networks have been getting themselves ready for this too, with new features and formats being developed – for example, Instagram buy buttons and the use of new formats such as Canvas and Collection ads on Facebook-owned networks that allow for more product-focused communication. It is hard to say how quickly adoption will happen in this space but all the signs are there for it to become far more commonplace than it is now.

REAL-TIME MARKETING

Ever since Oreo's marketing team released their now infamous 'Dunk in the Dark' tweet during the 2013 Super Bowl, real-time marketing on social has been at the top of the agenda for many social marketers. Of course, real-time agility is nothing new for PR professionals. 'Newsjacking', as it is sometimes known, is part and parcel of many PR campaigns and strategies – making a brand or business feel relevant and current by responding to the news agenda.

Oreo's success was fast and impactful, and led to numerous brands all trying to build social media war rooms to jump on the next unexpected opportunity. And, many brands came unstuck here – jumping on events that were neither appropriate for the brand – all in an effort to drive interaction with their content.

It feels as though we are starting to come full circle here. Marketers are realising that real-time marketing in itself might generate some short-term buzz but the business impact is usually hard to quantify. Just jumping on every 'trending topic' might give agencies and brands the opportunity to flex their creative muscle but is unlikely to lead to longer-term bottom line success. The shift of social media to a pay-to-play channel means that brands are usually unwilling to commit vast sums to always on activity – which is where real-time content tends to sit – so the content, which is usually resource intensive to create, struggles to get required return on investment.

But, some of the real-time marketing practices and approaches can still be useful. Rather than using insights into trends to create tactical content, these same insights can be a valuable way to plan and put together content strategies and plans. Taking an audience-first approach, where you use analytical tools and technologies to identify the topics and themes that are interesting your audience, is a valuable way to construct and plan meaningful content that intersects between your audience's interests and aspects that you as a brand have a right to play in. Some of this might result in fast-turnaround content but sometimes it will warrant larger – and longer – thinking.

BLOGGING AND ENTERPRISE NETWORKING

It is hard to remember, but blogging was the first form of social media that was really embraced by businesses and marketers. And, blogging still absolutely has a place for certain businesses, used in the right way.

But, with the arrival of other social platforms and content formats – combined with ever-increasing distractions that means user attention spans are less and less, blogs and blog content have been relegated. Blogs grew to be successful because of their ease of use. As the online self-publishing craze grew, blogs provided easy platforms to create and distribute content. These days, that same objective can be achieved in multiple different ways. Platforms like Medium and even LinkedIn Pulse offer new ways to create longer form, primarily written, content, but their usage is still relatively niche.

As ever, the secret to a successful blogging approach lies in effective distribution. It is not just enough to create the content – it needs to reach the intended audience too.

Another area of social network that, again, has promised much and yet often failed to deliver, is enterprise social networking. In previous years, technologies like Yammer offered businesses a way to move away from their reliance on email and offer more, social means to communicate within an organisation. However, the reliance on and pull of email is strong. And, often overly complex, these tools were always hard to deploy within a business and get user adoption.

There are signs that this might be starting to change. Facebook recently launched its own version – Workplace – which is essentially a closed version of the Facebook platform, designed for business. There is no need to learn any new technology, anyone that uses Facebook (and obviously, those numbers are pretty large) will easily be able to navigate the platform. Facebook is developing Workplace quickly and businesses are starting to explore its potential in a serious way.

While Workplace is not a silver bullet to save enterprise social networking, it is a glimpse of a hopeful future.

QUESTIONS

1. Where is your business on the road to social media maturity?

2. Are you still primarily posting organic content on social channels?

3. Are you embracing sophisticated audience targeting on social channels?

4. Have you audited the use (or potential use) of social media across your business?

5. Who are your social gatekeepers?

6. Do you have a social strategy and playbook?

7. Does your conversation calendar help you meet your strategic goals?

8. Are you taking a less is more approach to social content?

9. Are you embracing the new formats available on social channels?

10. How is your community management approach setup? Is it efficient?

11. How can social media add real value through conversion to your bottom line?

6

DIGITAL CONTENT AND CREATIVITY

If I received a pound coin every time someone told me that content is king in the marketing industry, I would be a very rich man. There is truth in it, of course, but all content is not created equal. Digital technologies have shifted the opportunity for content considerably. Never has creating engaging content been so easy. However, never has there been so much content out there to consume. As we have discussed before, the battle for attention is fierce online. As the opportunities to create better content increase, the bar for content that truly engages also rises.

THE BATTLE FOR STORIES

PR professionals should find themselves in a powerful place in the engagement space. PR is built upon the idea of earning attention through stories that people will find genuinely interesting, rather than the interruptive approach of traditional advertising. Interruption is over, engagement reigns and that brings a wealth of potential. The trouble is that earning attention is also the hardest thing to do.

The journalist used to be the gatekeeper. They were the one individual that stood between story and audience. They stood between creative idea and engagement with it. The experience of pitching to a journalist quickly tells you whether you have something that is really 'newsworthy' or not and you develop a good sixth sense for this. Get the phone slammed down on your pitch and you quickly work out how to craft a story that has legs.

However, digital distribution changes the balance. As more and more of our campaigns and programmes no longer have a journalist as a component, things change. Without that gatekeeper between brand and audience, the quality barrier is removed. It is tempting, without that potential deflector, to think that you can just push anything through. Often, the comms professional or agency is the one that has to stand in the middle and really assert the measure of quality. Is this story worthy of going out or not? Will this really add value to an audience or will it merely contribute, negatively, to the existing noise out there and, therefore, be less successful as a result?

Of course, ignoring the quality factor is a recipe for disaster. Therefore, the challenge is to still create, even when the journalistic checkpoint is removed, content that is worthy of earned engagement. Content that will really stop someone in their tracks – or, at least, stop their thumb scrolling through a feed. The aim is to create content that will meaningfully connect.

Of course, there are other barometers for success here – many of which we will consider in the measurement chapter 11. The challenge with 'engagement' metrics is that they are a relatively blunt instrument by which to judge whether a story or piece of content has resonated. A 'like' might be an indicator that something has resonated to some degree but it tells me very little about the commercial impact and is hardly aligned to business objectives.

Thus, while digital brings a clear need to be zero-focussed on content that will meaningfully translate, there are also a wealth of opportunities. The restrictions brought about by a small mobile screen are offset by the deeper, immersive potential.

LEAD CREATIVE AND MATCHING LUGGAGE

Another frequent barrier in the fight for good content is the aforementioned inter-agency dynamic. The traditional approach is that a lead creative agency will come up with a creative platform that then needs to be transported through marketing channels. In many consumer-facing situations, this often is best encapsulated in a TV commercial. However, TV scripts generally suffer from the syndrome identified above. There is no 'engagement filter' – it is an open goal for brand and agency to communicate a message and – more often than not (though there are notable counter examples too) – this ends up being content that is not truly engaging for an audience.

It is the same with other digital formats too. Take banner advertising. You buy some space and can put up anything you want (within reason). Again, the benchmark is low and success metrics often blunt.

Surely, it is time to change this outdated approach. In a world where interruptive marketing is decreasing in effectiveness across the board, there is surely an opportunity for earned media thinking to be at the heart of the creative idea. As Pepsi recently found out, when you create marketing content in a vacuum, you usually end up with something that just does not connect – at best – or, at worst, something that totally alienates.

The PR discipline is much more attuned to creative's role in culture and society. How do we shape our messages and our creative output to reflect the world of our audience? How do we ensure that we bear in mind the corporate reputation that might be under threat? How do we create an 'idea' that has deep and meaningful resonance, something that has true value?

It is against this framework that PR sits and, for this reason, I believe PR thinking has a role to play at the heart of creative development and expression.

THE VALUE OF INSIGHT AND STRATEGY

Data is often part of the solution here. Never have we worked in a space where it was so easy to take the pulse of the nation – or a particular audience segment. In days gone by, we would have meticulously read all the media we could get our hands on to tease out what is newsworthy; to try to jump on the current agenda and see what is making people tick. Now, it is easier than ever to do this through processes such as social listening or online conversation analysis.

If you want to see how people are talking around a particular topic, you can. Then, it is possible to target these people with relevant content as a result.

THE GROWTH OF PR CREATIVES

As we have discussed already, traditionally, PR has been a generalist career path where practitioners would wear multiple hats to get things done – from strategy, creative and execution. Digital has started to shift this. A digital approach requires generalists to be specialists in too many areas and thus bringing in more dedicated, deeper skill sets is an ongoing trend in the industry. Moreover, creatives sit at the heart of this. Increasingly, agencies – and even in-house teams – are hiring PR creatives to support a deeper and more dedicated approach to developing cut-through creative ideas.

It is a positive move. To cut through the noise and content clutter that exists, the creative output from a digital PR perspective must be better. However, there are dangers too. We must ensure that creative output continues to prioritise the earned, storytelling approach outlined above. It is easier to recruit creatives with a background that is not PR (which makes sense given that it is a relatively new specialism within the industry). However, it is important that we do not default to the interruptive marketing of the past and focus on telling compelling digital stories that resonate through the new channels we have at our disposal.

IMMERSIVE FORMATS

One of the reasons that dedicated creative support is useful is that it ensures that output stays at the forefront of the constantly changing digital ecosystem. Barely a week goes by when a digital or social platform does not announce a new format or feature. It is important that we make the most of these opportunities, but that means our creative and production resources need to be up-to-date with what is out there and know how to build these into campaigns.

Google's oft-cited '70/20/10 Model' is a good example of how to approach this. The idea is that 70% of what you do is tried and tested formats and approaches, 20% is evolving the 70% and 10% is pure innovation. This ensures that every campaign pushes boundaries and that it is done in a safe, easy-to-control way that does not put the entire budget at risk all the time.

It is also important to build in time. That's not always something that exists in an industry where speed of turnaround and agility is always to the fore. Innovating with new creative ideas and formats requires different skill sets that often take time to assemble and brief. Time is a key watch-out for PR creative in general. Usually, the creation of stand-out digital content will take more time and effort than PR campaign approaches of the past (apart from maybe organising an event). Therefore, building in time to really respond properly to a creative brief – both within an agency and in-house – is important.

WHY LESS IS MORE

The counterbalance to this and the potential saving grace, is that, often these days, 'less is more' when it comes to digital content. Social media is a perfect example, as we have seen. With paid media now a requirement for most social channels to get meaningful traction, it is better to invest more time and resources into creating better content than churning out conversation calendars with post after post. This plays into the idea of better creative craft; taking time to get the content right, rather than rushing to quantity over quality.

Data and analytics have a key role to play here too. Learning from how content performs, and then folding these insights into future content production, is an important way to guarantee that everything is optimised and that creative decisions are being made based on available facts. It is another area where digital has the advantage, being able to track content performance and evaluate whether something has engaged an audience. So ensuring this is properly linked into the creative process makes sure future content will continue to perform to the highest extent possible.

AGILE CONTENT CAPTURE

However, despite the need for quantity over quality, the agility that defines a lot of outstanding PR activities is still important to preserve. It is a key tenet of PR practice – understanding the news agenda and being able to react to its twists and turns by either changing course mid-campaign or coming up with something new, on-the-fly. As we have seen, the data now available through digital channels makes reactive content even easier to achieve. Social listening, for example, provides opportunities to see how conversations are changing and to amend a content approach as a result.

From a creative perspective, this requires structural agility – in the way creative and production teams are set up and operate – and agility and a willingness to amend creative ideas to flex. This is often hard for marketing teams used to crafting a TV commercial over many months. The idea that actually something can happen that requires plans to go out of the window or for new content to be approved and produced in hours is challenging.

It is important too, as we have discussed, not to get into the real-time marketing trap. It is very tempting for brands to jump on every bandwagon and every trending news story. Nevertheless, creative rigour is needed to ensure that content and campaigns still have brand values at the core.

THE PERILS OF NEWSROOMS

One of the new developments that have cropped up over the last few years, following Oreo's infamous 'Dunk in the Dark' real-time marketing moment at the Superbowl in 2013, is that brands have flocked to create permanent or one-off 'social newsrooms'. These are physical spaces that are set up, often with many TV screens displaying real-time information to help brands create reactive content.

There is a lot of value in this approach but the structure and process is important. So, is a clear idea of what the newsroom is looking to achieve – what does success look like? Too often, these situations result in lots of sub-standard content that gets low engagement. This ends up being resource-intensive and inefficient.

The reality is that a lot of 'real-time' content can actually be planned in advance. The Oreo example is perhaps one that really would have been hard to predict. Therefore, planning and rigor in the setup and planning phase are actually more important than a war-room filled with TV screens in terms of producing effective, business-benefitting content and campaigns.

It is also important that these approaches do not just focus on social media. Having PR practitioners, influencer strategists and even wider digital or advertising teams as part of this operation will ensure that real-time marketing is truly integrated and that multiple channels can be used.

UGC: PERILS AND REWARDS

The last area to consider and one that has grown significantly in recent years again is user generated content (UGC). As we have already discussed, often brands shoot themselves in the foot by trying to create content that totally misses the mark and feels out of place on social or digital channels. That is why the growth of influencer marketing – which we will examine in Chapter 7 – has been so readily accepted and used by communication and marketing professionals. It provides a way to create more authentic content that feels natural on these emerging channels.

The same is true of UGC and there are many brands and businesses out there that are now focussing their social content approach on the use of content created by their audiences.

There are a few elements to consider here. The first is that it is important to put a creative and brand or business filter across all UGC before it is reused. Although it is being created by the audience, it is important to ensure that content does not jar with communication messaging or visual identity. It is never going to be as close to these as brand-created content, but it is important not to let the balance tip too far the other way.

The other key thing to remember is seeking permission from the user before reusing content. Brands have become unstuck here and there are plenty of technologies out there now that allow this to be done quickly and easily.

QUESTIONS

1. How will you ensure that content is 'earned-worthy'?

2. How are you shaping content and creative output to reflect the world of your audience?

3. How are you using data to inspire content creation?

4. Do you have the right talent in place to compete creatively?

5. How is your team staying up to date with digital developments?

6. Are you still creating too much content?

7. Are data helping you to make creative and content decisions?

7

INFLUENCERS

The PR industry has always been in the business of influence. And, influence is as old as humankind is. It is a fundamental human trait. Throughout our lives, we frequently influence or are influenced, often subconsciously. The discipline of Public Relations is built upon the idea that not all influence is created equal. Some people are 'more influential' than others. They cause people to listen, to think and act in different ways. If we can channel this influence and get it to work in our favour, then the rewards are potentially great.

Generally, this is defined by status and method of message distribution. Influential people are more likely to be quoted in newspapers, feature on TV or make speeches to rooms full of people who, in turn, have influence over others.

Digital channels have turned this on its head. Status has been democratised. The web, and social channels in particular, gives anyone the ability to become influential to a far greater degree. Teenage girls in their bedrooms can create videos extolling the virtues of particular make-up, activists can build cult followings and employees can turn to social channels to influence or disrupt.

Influencer marketing against this new digital backdrop
has been quick to spring up and develop. Whole agencies and
in-house teams are now frequently dedicated to the process
and a whole industry of technology vendors have appeared.
And, inevitably, other disciplines outside PR, have started to
view influencer marketing as something they want a piece of.
Media agencies and ad shops are increasingly seeing influencer marketing as something they should have a say over.
Much of this has been driven by the professionalism of the
influencer space, with many influencers – with big and small
reach – now commanding financial returns for partnerships
with brands and businesses.

But, for me, a lot of this misses the point of the value
of influence. The reason why PR has always centred itself
around influencers is because of third-party validation. It is
far more impressive for someone else to tell you that I am
great than if I tell you myself. It brings (usually) authenticity
and transparency. It is a recommendation that speaks with
more weight and potency. It might be bought but it still must
come from a place of truth. 'Faking it' only diminishes the
power of the influencer and the trust their audiences place on
them. Influence needs to be earned – both by the influencer
and the brand.

THE PROFESSIONALISATION OF INFLUENCE

The rise of digital distribution methods for influencers
puts all of this under threat and I firmly believe we are at a
time when the role and effectiveness of influencers for marketing is under threat. And, there is no clear solution to this
problem.

Inevitably, at a time when influencer marketing is seen to
be at its most powerful, businesses and brands have piled on.

On the other side of the coin, influencers have unprecedented opportunities to grow significant audiences through digital channels. And, with it, they now have brands and businesses knocking at their doors with offers of significant investment. To cope with this influx, many influencers now have agents and many have now entered into complex exclusivity agreements with brands across all kinds of sectors. This is most prevalent in consumer lifestyle sectors – for example, beauty and travel – but is quickly coming into all areas of activity, including corporate and business-to-business.

This is a perfect storm. Influencers are more powerful than ever. And, they are more appealing to brands and businesses than ever before too. The temptation is significant on both sides. And, so, are the risks.

On the influencer side, you have a situation where it is easy to over-extend. I have seen examples of Instagrammers where every other post is a brand partnership. I have also seen examples where influencers have been totally rejected by their audiences because they are seen as being in the pocket of their paymasters; the brands.

On the brand side, if you are just paying influencers for reach, you risk compromising them (and therefore yourself) but you also risk tainting your brand with associations that do not work. The art of influencer marketing has been in identifying the right influencer to work with. With the commercialisation of the industry, a lot of that has disappeared.

THE AUTHENTICITY BALANCE

At the heart of all this is a finely tuned authenticity balance. Influencers need to retain authenticity in the eyes of their fans and followers. If the number one reason for following an influencer versus a celebrity is that they are more 'like me', then ensuring this sense of peer-to-peer remains is crucial. Stray too far one way and the authenticity balance disappears.

For brands, the same is true. If a beauty blogger starts talking all of a sudden about the value of weed killer, then the authenticity balance is immediately out of skew. And, this will be to the detriment of both influencer and brand.

It is a requirement on both sides to keep the authenticity balance in check. And, there are a number of ways to ensure this happens:

- *Topic relevance* – It is understandable that brands will often want to use influencers that have audiences that extend beyond their core, but you need to ensure there is always a link to what they 'talk' about on a regular basis and that this does not stray too far.

- *Brand fit* – The same is true of brand fit. Some brands, even if the topic relevance is close, just should not work with certain influencers – the 'fit' just is not there.

- **The ask** – Sometimes the influencer and brand partnership feel like a perfect fit but what the influencer is being asked to do feels totally out of keeping with what the influencer usually does on their channel. Authenticity immediately disappears.

THE RISE OF DATA AND IMPORTANCE OF IDENTIFICATION

One of the most critical elements of influencer marketing is therefore identification of the right influencers. This is another area that has radically changed since the onset of digital channels and is also an area where data has come to the fore. But, here too there is danger.

The biggest danger when it comes to influencer marketing is obsession with reach figures. It is not uncommon for the first question I receive when speaking to a client is for them to ask how many followers the influencer in question has. It is always the wrong question.

The first reason for this is that follower numbers are not generally a very powerful metric for predicting success. Take a prominent beauty blogger that has 10 million fans. There is so much that is unknown in that number. How many of those fans are people I am looking to reach? How many of them are fake? How many of them are engaged with the influencer on a regular basis?

The second reason that follower numbers are proving less and less useful is that they tell you very little about the power of the influencer to get their audience to act in a particular way. Depending on the objectives of your campaign, you will likely want influencers that encourage an audience to do something specific. You might just want broad awareness, but you might want to start conversation or encourage an audience to click through and buy. For each of these objectives, you will want an influencer that behaves – and causes his or her audience to behave – in a different, though specific way.

All the data to inform these decisions now exists. It is possible to gather so much more data about an influencer above and beyond the number of followers they have, that I am constantly amazed how infrequently this is done.

The technology that has built up around influencer marketing is significant. From the cheap to the expensive, from the simple to the complex, there is a product out there promising to solve any influencer problem you might have. And yet, there is danger here that needs to be cautioned against. Off-the-shelf tools are just that. They appear simple and straightforward on the surface – you type in your keyword and you get a ready-made list of influencers. But, make sure you interrogate what is under the hood. Many of these tools are not transparent about how they analyse and rank influencers – so you are basing decisions on blind faith.

They are all usually also one-size-fits-all solutions. So, if brand A types in a keyword and gets a list of influencers, that list will be exactly the same as the list that brand B has received when they typed in exactly the same keyword. Which totally goes against everything we have already talked about in terms of the importance of finding influencers that not only fit your brand or business, but also the objectives of your particular campaign or piece of activity. It is never as simple as a technology would have you believe.

The answer then is to properly interrogate the solutions you are using but then also remember that the list you receive is probably only part of the answer. In an ideal world, you would be able to do your only analysis. But, at the least, make sure you interrogate every influencer to ensure they really are the right influencer for the job.

Sometimes, this is a very easy thing to do. For example, say you are a coffee brand – have you checked that the influencers you are targeting actually like coffee?

INFLUENCERS ARE NOT JOURNALISTS

Outreach is the next stage in the journey. When social influencer marketing was still in its infancy, the challenge was how to communicate with people that did not subscribe to the same unspoken rules as journalists. How do you share information with someone that probably does not know what an embargo is and that would probably not keep it even if they did?

The reality is that sending a press release to a list of influencers just will not work (not that it necessarily even does for journalists these days). Instead, crafting an individual outreach, tailored to their content, approach, platform and interests is key, even more so than it is with journalists.

As influencers have become more 'professional' in their approach, this has morphed slightly. As money has started to change hands – and whenever it does – the relationship becomes more contractual in nature. Negotiating with an influencer is not always easy but is absolutely crucial to ensure that the necessary safeguards are put in place. Here are some of the elements that really do need to be taken into account:

- *Deliverables* – How many posts/pieces of content do you expect them to deliver and on which channels?

- *Timescales* – When does activity need to be live (be as specific as possible)?

- *Approval* – Do you need to see content and sign it off before posting?

- *Whitelisting* – Do you want to have the option to put paid media behind their content? Most networks need you to prove permission before you can do this.

- *Use of paid media* – Will you be putting paid media behind their content on your own channels?

- *Use of content* – How is their content to be used? On your social channels? Through other marketing? Over what period of time?

- *Content criteria* – Be specific about any content criteria; right down to the hashtags you want them to use and links you want them to add.

- *Data access* – Often, you will only be able to access certain metrics without having access to an influencer's analytics dashboards, so make sure you ask for it.

Most influencers – and certainly agents – will be used to being asked the above questions and integrating them into contracts. But, you might be expected to pay more for some of the elements as part of a negotiation.

DECLARING INTEREST

Another result of the professionalism of influencer marketing and the move towards a financial value exchange is that regulators, like the Advertising Standards Authority (ASA) are starting to pay far more attention to the use of influencers for commercial gain. It has always been best practice to flag where an influencer has been paid to promote a product or service – much in the same way that advertorials were always specified clearly to an audience. But now in many markets around the world, this is increasingly a requirement with failure to follow resulting in financial penalties.

As the ASA says itself,

> 'Hidden' advertising on social media is taking up more and more of our time. In particular, marketing by influencers is an increasing challenge and one that doesn't fit so neatly into our standard categories." (ASA, 2017)

In the United Kingdom, under the UK Code of Non-broadcast Advertising and Direct & Promotional Marketing, responsibility for disclosing an 'ad' (anything with a financial value exchange – for example, money, a gift or a perk) lies with the brand. The solution to this is to ensure that the content in question is clearly labelled as being an advert, usually with an identifier such as #ad or, increasingly through dedicated 'paid promotion' tagging on social platforms themselves.

It is easy to see – especially in the case of influencers, whose usage really stemmed from the 'earned' media space – how the use of identifiers such as #ad might not be welcomed by comms professionals. But, it is absolutely a requirement of influencer marketing these days and should never be overlooked. Regulators like the ASA are starting to take action and the negative brand association can be significant if not followed.

COLLABORATION AND CO-CREATION

The primary reason for using influencers as part of a campaign or programme of activity is the authenticity that they bring. It is therefore confusing when I see brands clearly asking influencers to 'do' something they feel uncomfortable with or create content that is clearly inconsistent with their usual output. As money starts to change hands with the influencer relationship, it is easy to see how influencer might start to be used in a dictatorial way. Generally, my experience is that the opposite is always the best approach.

The reason we use influencers is because they have already demonstrated that they can open up and develop a loyal following. They have built a community of people that are engaged in what they create or say. Any attempts to go against this feels like a waste of time, resources and money.

It is also easy to see how this might come about during the course of the creation of a campaign. In a traditional PR campaign, outreach and engagement with a journalist is often the last thing to happen. But, treat influencers in the same way and you will end up with content that fails to connect with their audience. It takes courage to do it, but the best approach is to involve the influencers you are planning to use in the ideation phase of the campaign. Do not go to them with a finished idea; go to them with an objective and a jumping off point. Leave them to fill in the details and come back with creative suggestions. The result will be a campaign that not only more effectively delivers a message, but also one that more deeply resonates with the target audience.

INFLUENCERS AS CONTENT CREATORS

Building on this approach is another trend that is growing in popularity and that is using influencers as content creators. It is easy to see how this has come about. Creating content for owned social channels can be time and resource intensive. And, the results are not always well suited to the platform. Brands have shown, time and time again, that they do not lend themselves to being great social content creators.

Influencers on the other hand do exactly that. They have built their success on creating newsfeed-first content that brands and businesses want to truly engage with.

So, more and more brands are turning to influencers to do the hard work for them. Seeing them as the perfect source of social creative input. Many are not even asking the influencers to post the content on their channels; they just want the imagery or video to use on the brand's own social accounts. It will not work for all businesses, but will be a perfect avenue to cost-effective, social-first content for others.

BUILDING INFLUENCERS FROM WITHIN

It is often easiest to see how influencers have a role to play for consumer brands but it is actually often more powerful for business-to-business or corporate campaigns. Here, influence tends to be easier to identify, if not always as easy to achieve. Money is less likely to change hands and the role of offline is likely to play a bigger role. But, there are a number of techniques that are making the use of influencers in campaigns like this much more attractive. In the paid media chapter 9 , we will look at how targeted advertising can be used to reach smaller groups of people with highly targeted messages and how this can really help the effectiveness of corporate campaigns.

Then, there is the role of influencers that you might already have in your brand or business. I remember speaking to a company in the healthcare sector that had strictly told its internal employees never to mention the brand on social media, partly because of the regulatory headaches and potential reputational issues that might occur. They eventually had a light-bulb moment when they realised that their employee base was actually highly tapped into the professional communities they were looking to reach out to, and that any regulatory or reputational risks were worth it, and they quickly put in place a training and empowerment programme. We will look at this internal role more in the corporate chapter 10, but it is worth remembering that influence often lies within.

Another area we will explore in more detail is creating thought leaders that can build up positions of influence (or reassert existing influence) from within a business and, again, this is an area of influencer marketing that digital channels have made easier than ever before.

Of course, as discussed right at the beginning of this chapter, all of this depends on having a very clear objective at the outset. What is influencer marketing looking to achieve for the business and how will this be realised? However, when this is all in place, influencers are perhaps the biggest weapon at the disposal of any modern digital PR professional.

QUESTIONS

1. How are influencers currently playing a role?

2. How do you keep the authenticity balance in check?

3. Are you using data to inform influencer identification?

4. Are reach figures alone driving decisions about influencer selection?

5. What is your process for identifying influencers? Can it be optimised?

6. Are you contracting in the right way with influencers?

7. Are you meeting all requirements to disclose influencer partnerships?

8. Are you co-creating with influencers as part of the creative process?

8

DIGITAL MARKETING

Clearly, it is not only in the PR discipline where digital has had a transformative effect on the world of marketing. As consumer behaviour shifts and online activities begin to take up more and more of our daily lives, it is no surprise that marketers have shifted their focus. However, it is perhaps surprising in many ways, how slow this shift has actually been. While a significant proportion of media spend is now going through digital pipes, offline channels – especially TV – still dominate marketing plans. There are many of reasons for this. Some of it is due to legacy approaches, some is due to concerns over the accuracy of digital metrics and some of it is just down to new channels proving their worth.

Elements like digital banner advertising are starting to struggle as consumer behaviour rails against it and technologies such as ad blockers start to take hold. However, there are plenty of digital marketing activities that are now commonplace for any marketer, no matter what sector or audience focus – email marketing, Customer Relationship Management (CRM), search – all areas that have proven value and increasing levels of sophistication. There is no doubt that, as with digital PR, the future will be dominated by these new approaches and the word 'digital' will, essentially, become redundant. How quickly this occurs is the unanswered question at the moment.

THE BLURRED LINES

Therefore, what impact does this have on the communication and PR professional? As ever, there are increasing blurred lines, which are becoming significant. On the one hand, you can look at elements of digital marketing services that might be beneficial to a more traditional PR campaign – and we will discuss these in the following paragraphs. Then, there is the viewpoint of looking at broader campaigning and ensuring that digital PR approaches are integrated with digital marketing activities. It is this latter approach that will probably occur more often but it is the first approach, that we will tackle first, that is potentially the most interesting for the modern digital PR practitioner.

As mentioned earlier, there are likely to be blurred lines in terms of roles and responsibilities here, with in-house teams and all with agency loop teams. Thus, unpicking these and ensuring lines are clearly drawn, but collaboration is to the fore, will be absolutely vital. We will look at this more when we come to examine the structures of PR and marketing teams. In time, much of this will die away as teams are more used to running campaigns that straddle multiple disciplines, but it remains a part and parcel of digital activities these days.

THE SEARCH ENGINE MARKETING (SEO) 'MISS'

The PR industry – in the United Kingdom, at least – has generally been seen to be slow to adopt digital. There is also a generally held belief that the industry – and practitioners in general – missed the opportunity (and still have in many cases) that organic search offered, in particular as an additional revenue stream for agencies.

As 'search' started to boom as a way for consumers to navigate online content, there also grew an opportunity for marketers to capitalise on this for brands and businesses in order to ensure that they stayed front of mind. Although search is in many ways a marketing discipline, the practicalities of organic search marketing – at least in the early days – dovetailed with PR very closely. As search algorithms were focussed primarily around authenticity and trust, this felt like an own goal for PR to show its worth. 'Link-building' as a practice felt as though it was something that was well suited to PR techniques. Secure 'coverage' online and ensure there was a link back to a brand's website, and in turn you would get an organic search boost.

It is easy to see how this would have been an obvious opportunity to unite two disciplines in a mutually beneficial way. However, the closest the industry really came was 'optimising' a press release for search and including keywords and links. This approach nodded to the importance of search and ignored some of the additional complexities and technicalities that were involved in the emerging discipline of search engine marketing.

Much of this is down to the challenges around skill sets. Sure, it is possible to teach traditional PR professionals how to modify their approach to benefit search, but a full search engine marketing campaign would require new skill sets around web development, for example, that just were not in existence within most PR teams or agencies. The two approaches just did not neatly align and so, in many businesses, the two developed separately. PR remained with the comms team and search marketing developed within 'digital' teams in-house and dedicated search agencies started to appear. In many ways, this is still the case today. Although search algorithms have evolved beyond pure link building as a signal, there is still a lot of value in the two approaches working hand in hand. The reality is that within many businesses, this just still is not the case.

DIGITAL SERVICES AS PART OF A PR CAMPAIGN

The first way in which digital marketing is relevant to a digital PR approach is by integrating digital marketing activities within PR campaigns. It is pretty easy to do but it does require a slightly different approach and mindset.

For example, imagine you are running a PR campaign to build the thought leadership profile of a company's CEO. It is easy to think of the myriad of PR techniques – old and new – that you would employ to achieve this, whether blog posts, bylines, press releases, speaker opportunities, media interviews, etc. However, it is also not hard to think about digital marketing channels that might be able to benefit this objective – for example, emailing relevant thought leadership content to 'influential' people or customers on the company's CRM database. Or, creating a search (organic and/or paid) campaign to ensure that any searches for a particular topic resulted in links to the content that has been created. There is also the opportunity to link digital advertising in too – for example, retarget anyone that came to the blog post that has been created, with adverts that relate to the thought leadership topic and then drive the individual more of a hard-conversion point on the company website.

BUILDING A CUSTOMER JOURNEY

This last point is a pretty important example of how integrating digital marketing services into a PR campaign can really start to benefit everyone involved. In addition, a key building block to unlocking this is a clear understanding of the customer journey and the role that every channel is playing across it – as we discussed when we looked at digital ecosystems. All digital marketing channels have a role to play – including digital PR ones – but the role will change from audience to audience and from campaign to campaign – often, depending on the job to be done and the overall objective.

In the example above, would a digital advert have been as powerful had the person seeing it not read the thought leadership article before?

It is why an integrated strategic approach, which includes all stakeholders, is vital as a starting point. Fundamentally, this requires us not seeing things as channel-led or tactic-led but objective- or audience-led. Approached in this way, you begin to build multi-layered campaigns that integrate different marketing disciplines and are all working together to achieve a clear goal – something that we'll come on to discuss in the chapter 11 on measurement.

PROVING VALUE

Ultimately – again, as in the example above – much of this allows us to then prove the value that digital (or non-digital) PR activities are helping to contribute to. How much better to be able to talk about the conversions that resulted from the remarketing campaign as opposed to just the number of hits to the blog post? Again, to achieve this, a more complicated campaign approach and a detailed customer journey is required, alongside real collaboration within the business or between agencies for it to be realised.

The key takeaway here for digital PR professionals is to be constantly thinking about how digital marketing tactics and techniques could extend a campaign and add additional value – or at least demonstrate this value in real-terms above and beyond engagement. For the PR industry – where providing ROI and real business value has always been a challenge, whether real or inferred – surely, this approach and potential are just too good to let slip.

There are dangers here, of course. How do you show the value of each different channel when many are involved in delivering that last conversion point? Last click attribution – where the credit is given to the channel that provided the final click-through – rather than acknowledging those that went before – is generally being seen these days as a poor way to provide ROI figures to marketing channels, for obvious reasons, but it is still not easy and it is often hard to demonstrate tangible value for an interaction that occurred far up the marketing funnel and may or may not have been a key contributor to the final conversion point.

THE CHANGING ROLE OF A WEBSITE

One of the areas where PR and digital marketing most frequently overlap is around websites and other digital destinations. Creating landing pages that become a focal point for PR campaigns is a tried and tested approach that often delivers value. However, it is amazing how often this does not happen. I have often seen a great piece of traditional PR coverage in a newspaper, for example, only to go and visit the company's website to find absolutely nothing about the announcement or campaign. At best, you can often hunt down the press release, but that hardly does a good job of furthering someone's interest in a story, when they have demonstrated so much proactivity on their part to go and look for it.

Too often, we are focussed on a final output rather than a business outcome. A piece of coverage – offline or online – should only be the start of a relationship between audience and brand, not the beginning and end. Moreover, a website can be a powerful vehicle for this.

The role of a website has changed significantly over the last few years and, in many ways, will depend on the sector in which you are working. For many businesses – where ecommerce is now alive and well – a company website is *the* place where business is carried out – it is absolutely vital. For others a website is merely a place where interested parties can find out more about a corporate entity but does not actually include much of substance and does not warrant significant investment by the company itself.

A lot of this changing, however. Ecommerce is starting to move to platforms – as we have discussed already – with major players like Amazon becoming a focus and even platforms like Facebook offering opportunities. Even on the corporate side, the idea that the website is always the go-to place for information about a business is starting to change, with destinations such as LinkedIn, Wikipedia or Glassdoor often getting the click ahead of a business's domain. As the audience behaviour evolves, we need to be constantly examining the role that digital platforms play in our PR and marketing strategies and your website is just one example of where this is happening already.

PR AS A CONTRIBUTOR TO THE MARKETING MIX

This has already been touched on but it is worth pulling out in its own right too – the role that PR activities can have in the wider digital marketing funnel. For example, imagine you have run a product review programme for a new consumer technology product. This has resulted in a number of great reviews in technology and lifestyle publications as well as inclusion in a number of lifestyle blogs. This is all content that can be utilised across digital channels – to customers via emails, flagged on the company website or on product pages on an ecommerce site.

It is a simple example but a clear one that shows the value between PR and digital marketing can be two-way. There is plenty of opportunity for PR professionals to use digital marketing to benefit the result of PR campaigns and an opportunity for digital marketers to integrate PR content in their own channels and approaches. As ever, collaboration and integration are key to making this a reality and building value for the brand or business.

QUESTIONS

1. How are you clarifying the roles and responsibilities of different disciplines?

2. Are you making the most of organic search opportunities and the link with PR?

3. How can digital marketing techniques add value to the PR activities you are running?

4. Is everyone aligned with the same goal and objective?

5. Can digital marketing help to prove the value of PR activities?

6. Are your PR activities reflected in the content your audience will find on your other digital properties?

7. What is the role of your website?

9

PAID MEDIA

In the days before digital, a chapter about paid media in a book about public relations would certainly have seemed out of place. Apart from perhaps dabbling in advertorials or paying a celebrity for endorsement, most traditional PR approaches did not generally include forms of paid advertising. PR is an earned media discipline. It has always relied on the power of convincing someone to write, talk or think about a company, person or idea in a different way. It is the power of earned media influence that made PR the vital discipline it is today and why so many businesses around the world invest in it.

But, as we have seen, digital changes everything. And, paid media is perhaps the starkest example of this. Paid is not a nice-to-have in modern PR. It is not something that can be selected – or not. It is a requirement to any successful campaign and, more than this, it is a fantastic technique to help reach an audience in a powerful, disruptive way.

There remains a stigma around paid media in the industry, however. There are some that see it as 'cheating'. The fact that it is no longer a nice-to-have but an imperative, makes this argument futile. The other challenge that many often face – both in-house and within agencies – is that traditional PR budgets are just not set up for paid media campaigns and the investments (although not always significant) that they require. In traditional business budgeting (where last year's budget is essentially copied and tweaked), there are substantial challenges for internal comms and PR teams that want to make paid media a key part of their new PR approach.

It is rightly important that teams are able to justify these additional investments and it is highly likely that usual PR metrics such as coverage just will not cut it when paid budgets are at stake. As we will see in this chapter, modern PR is alive and well and paid media can make it impactful like never before.

THE DEATH OF PESO

For years now, people have talked about PESO – paid, earned, shared and owned. For even longer, marketing disciplines have often (apart from shared) been defined in these terms. PR was always seen as an earned media discipline. The reality is that these terms are unhelpful. They suggest that you can merely group things together in neat silos. They suggest that each operates individually, separated from each other. PESO masks what is a complex media environment, when you cannot divide what is paid, what is earned.

Unfortunately, this mindset is so entrenched within marketing (and broader business practices) that it is hard to counter. It is not that a channel or piece of content cannot be divided into one of these brackets, they can. It is just that often the power of a piece of content lies in it being used across multiple silos. It starts as earned, is then boosted by paid and this triggers a large viral impact through shares. In the end, it is impossible to label it and the success it has achieved is exactly the opposite of siloed thinking.

In the modern digital ecosystem, we need to be integrated and joined up in the way we approach content and marketing in general to ensure that we are making the most of every channel and making the most of the different ways in which they can now be used.

THE ARGUMENT FOR PAID MEDIA

Making an argument for paid media is not going to be easy for many comms professionals. As mentioned earlier, it is not within the DNA of most comms – or even marketing – teams. For me, there are a few stages and different ways to approach building an argument. The first – and we will talk about this more in the following – is to frame the rationale in shifting trends in consumer behaviour; bring it back to macro trends that will be understandable and recognisable across the board.

The second part of the argument is to focus on results. Show what is possible to achieve with and without paid. Show how the initial investment in PR activities – whether content, planning resource, media outreach, etc. – can be boosted with paid media. If you are going to invest £x anyway, then why not try and extract maximum impact, which will provide a greater return.

The final approach that I always advocate is testing to prove the business case. The great thing about paid media on digital channels – unlike offline – is that generally the barriers to entry are incredibly low. It is easy to test a campaign with a small budget to prove effectiveness. You do not need to sign off significant budgets to start with. Start small. Prove it works. And then, use the arguments to scale.

PAY TO PLAY

Paid media brings significant benefits by helping to achieve greater impact and reach. But, in certain areas, paid media is now a requirement. It is a pay to play world and those that ignore this fact are just shooting themselves in the foot. Social media is the perfect example here. On many social networks, as we have discussed already, paid media is the only solution to ensure that you reach people. Facebook is the prime example, but it is starting to become the norm across other platforms too. While some brands still manage to achieve decent organic results, others are experiencing next to nothing – and both will certainly benefit from the boost that paid media brings.

It is easy to see, again, how securing budget to put into social media will be hard. When you have got something that you have been enjoying for some time without having to use additional paid media budgets, then it is easy to see how making the case for additional investment will be hard. Social media hurts even more. For years, the likes of Facebook spoke about the need to build up (often using paid media) big followings on brand Pages only for marketers to then be asked to pay again to reach them. This leaves a bad taste in the mouth but there isn't really a way out. You have to be in it to win it.

This has also brought around the situation where brands have developed two types of social media teams – those managing organic and those managing paid. This is yet again another example of where PESO makes little sense. These teams should be unified with a common goal and with the objective of making social media as a channel as effective as possible.

AN EARNED APPROACH TO PAID MEDIA

Of course, the rush to paid media does not mean we throw the baby out with the bathwater. Paid media adoption does not mean that PR merely becomes advertising. It is a danger that is worth really mobilising against. It is easy to use paid media to be lazy. To view it as an opportunity to deliver a message rather than to engage in a meaningful way. As I have said all along, interruptive marketing is dying. An earned media approach to digital storytelling is the only way forward and using paid media should change that approach.

One way to think about this is through taking an earned media approach to paid. This is a philosophical approach but can also be a practical one. Philosophically, if you judge every piece of content on it is earned-worthiness, then that is pretty good way to judge whether it is likely to succeed. Whether you end up putting paid media behind it or not, it has passed the 'journalist test' (i.e. would a journalist slam down the phone on you if you tried to sell this in?).

But, there is a practical method to this too. If using social, you actually put content out organically (or with small paid media support) to start with and then look at its performance, this is a great way to plan media spend based on what is getting 'earned' traction rather than mindlessly putting your whole paid media budget against every post equally.

Viewed in this way, an earned approach to paid media can become the solution to fight against siloed PESO thinking and achieve the best of both worlds simultaneously.

THE POWER OF TARGETING

The other main argument to support investment in paid media, especially through digital channels, is to make the most of the myriad of targeting options that are now available. With the rise of programmatic ad buying, you can be sure that your content is getting in front of the right people at the right time. This can be incredibly powerful for all types of PR campaigning and is obviously far more efficient.

It can get even more sophisticated than that too. With lookalike audiences, you can take segments of people – for example, a list of influencers you think could hold sway on Twitter. You can then use Twitter (and other networks) to find other people that match this profile – lookalike audiences – and then deliver content to them in a targeted way. You can even 'dark post' this content so that is does not appear to everyone, just to the selected group. Scale this and you can deliver tailored messages to different audience segments at scale across a campaign.

Match that to the earned approach to paid outlined above (essentially, ensuring you are sending content that they will want to consume and engage with) and you have a very powerful way to be focussed and efficient in your distribution approach. As with the example above, this is not useful for awareness campaigns where reaching the right people – and lots of them – is important, but can be incredibly useful in targeted campaigns where actually the group of people you need to reach is relatively small.

USING PAID MEDIA TO BOOST PR

As we have seen, paid media is not an either/or option these days. It works best when it is part of an integrated campaign. Indeed, if you have got a traditional PR campaign with good results then paid media can be used as an effective way to extend the reach and duration of this campaign and ensure you get maximum returns from your initial PR activities.

One of the easiest ways to do this is through syndication of content. Either through syndication platforms – of which more and more now exist. Or by repurposing the editorial

coverage and putting out links to it on owned channels, supported by paid media. It really does make a lot of sense. If you
get a piece of coverage in a publication, then that does a great
job of reaching some of the people that subscribe to or read
that publication on a regular basis. But, unless you are in a
very targeted industry where all the people you want to reach
are pretty likely to be reading that one publication, then the
chances are that this one piece of coverage will not reach the
entire audience.

An earned piece of coverage has a significant amount of
authenticity and credibility, so making sure that you utilise
this powerful asset and reach as many relevant people with it
as possible is sensible. So, the syndicated approach outlined
earlier is a very useful tactic and a great way to combine traditional PR approaches with paid media.

When it comes to social channels, there is another powerful argument and that is that time and time again, 'earned-
worthy' content sees greater organic and viral traction when
boosted with paid media. It seems counterintuitive but it
actually makes total sense when you think it through. Most
viral and organic engagement on social channels happens
when lots of people like something and the algorithm gives it
a boost as a result or people share the content which then has
a domino effect. If you have a piece of content that is generating high engagement or shares, then it stands to reason that
the more people you expose to it, the more engagement (and
algorithmic boost) and shares you are likely to get. So, the
content performs better and you get more organic traction
that you would have received without paid media.

Again, these are just further examples of how paid and
earned work most powerfully these days when they are working together. They increase the results of pieces of content and
ensure that you are able to get in front of the people you want
to reach.

Another area that is worth touching on here, although we will explore it further in future chapters too, is the use of paid media around crisis communication and issues management. This is an area that is often beset with challenges and a paid media approach is not always the right one. But if you are in a situation, for example, where something has happened and you need to ensure you are able to get fast, accurate information out to the right people, then using paid media – for example, paid search – to ensure that you get the message you want to convey in front of an audience makes a lot of sense and can be a very powerful tool to have in the arsenal.

INFLUENCERS AND MEDIA PARTNERSHIPS

As we have discussed earlier, there are now areas where paid media plays a role but the boundaries are blurred. Influencer marketing is a good example of this, where many influencers these days will want to be paid to engage with a business or a brand around a particular campaign. And it is not only the initial contract, but also potentially the paid media support that then needs to go behind the content in question once it has been created. There are some interesting emerging techniques here too, such as whitelisting – where you can put paid media budget behind content that has been created by an influencer without reposting the content on your owned channels.

The traditional media are starting to blur the boundaries now too. Many publishers have commercial teams that are not just focussed on advertising but on selling partnership opportunities with brands and businesses. This is something that we are seeing in a big way with some of the new digital publishers such as Vice and Buzzfeed. But, even traditional players such as the BBC and *The Guardian* have big branded content teams. It is not uncommon these days for PR pitches to editorial teams to be forwarded onto the branded content team who will come back with a partnership and sponsorship opportunity.

Again, traditional PR approaches would dictate that this is not an effective way to use PR resources, but true partnership and co-creation – as with influencers – can often be a really powerful tactic or technique. Especially with publications like Vice and Buzzfeed who have big teams of social-first content creators that can help build campaign content that will really resonate with their audiences. The boundaries are blurred but are not likely to get any clearer any time soon, so this is definitely an area to bear in mind for campaigning.

CHALLENGES WITH PAID MEDIA

Finally, it would not be possible to talk about paid media these days without touching on some of the challenges that face the industry at the moment. For a while now, there have been significant concerns raised about the transparency of digital advertising and the rise of bot traffic. Some estimate now that a significant proportion of impressions through advertising are not generated by human interactions.

There is significant concern out there in the industry that is starting to force some of the big players – such as Facebook and Google – to take steps to upgrade their platforms and reassure big advertisers. As P&G's Marc Pritchard said in January 2017,

> *We have an antiquated media buying and selling system that was clearly not built for this technology revolution. We serve ads to consumers through a non-transparent media supply chain with spotty*

> *compliance to common standards unreliable*
> *measurement hidden rebates and new inventions*
> *like bot and methbot fraud. (Campaign, 2017)*

The digital advertising world is ripe for revolution. Not only is hard to trust the metrics, but the formats that exist are also quickly becoming less and less effective. Too often, it feels as though we have taken offline formats – such as TV advertising – and merely converted them to the digital and social space, rather than thinking afresh and creating forms of advertising that really add value to the way we use digital platforms. This is not going to happen overnight but it is definitely high up the agenda of the major advertising platforms.

Ad blocking is another trend that will only speed up this shift. While ad blocking the United Kingdom is still relatively low, it is scaling quickly in the United States and many browsers and phone operating systems will soon come with ad blockers built in. This may well sound a death knell for traditional display advertising and, while social ads have mostly avoided detection to date, this is likely to shift as the technology becomes smarter.

None of the above is a reason – currently – not to engage in paid media activities through digital channels. But, it is definitely a space to watch closely and, as mentioned, is one that is likely to see innovation in the near future.

QUESTIONS

1. How is paid media playing a role in your activities?

2. How are you building a business case – rooted in data – to support paid media investment?

3. Are you utilising paid media across all social activities?

4. How can targeting help you reach the right audience at the right time?

5. Can paid media help you boost traditional PR results?

6. How is paid and earned working hand in hand to deliver better results?

7. Are you tapping into partnership opportunities as part of campaigns?

8. How are you ensuring that there is transparency in the metrics you are collecting around paid media usage?

10

CORPORATE AND B2B

It is easy to think about digital PR and assume that this is immediately more suited to businesses and brands in the consumer arena. But, some of the most meaningful digital PR activities I have undertaken have been for business-to-business (B2B) brands or within the corporate PR space. There is good reason for this. With consumer brands, you are often targeting large or mass audiences. Digital lends itself to this in many ways but it does not play to its strengths. The other challenge with consumer brands is that they do not always own the digital journey from awareness to conversion.

Contrast this with businesses targeting businesses. Often, the audiences are relatively small or at least highly targeted. Digital channels come into their own here, giving you a cost-effective way to reach people who you know are going to be interested in your products or services. And, because businesses operating in this space often control the lead generation aspect of what they do, it is far easier with digital channels to show how marketing and PR activity has taken a customer or prospect through the journey and the impact that content or particular tactics have had as a result.

So, while it is easy to think consumer-first when looking at the digital space, as we will see in this chapter, it is often businesses that are looking to target specific audiences in a very specific way that have most to gain from a focus and investment in digital PR.

THE POWER OF TARGETING

Targeting absolutely lies at the heart of this. Fundamentally, we share a lot of information about ourselves on digital platforms. Often, these platforms will know who we are, where we work, our job title and potentially also passions and interests. Again, the default assumption is that most of this relates to what we do as consumers, but it is just as applicable to our professional lives. The boundaries between personal and professional have simply disappeared online. We are just as likely to start a search for a professional supplier with a Google search as we are when looking for our next consumer purchase.

And, this wealth of information that now exists online about who we are and what we do professionally is massively beneficial from a marketing and PR standpoint. This is not only in terms of lead generation, but also in terms of building reputation, thought-leadership and deriving an insight.

Social listening or conversation analysis is a great case in point. Want to know how a particular topic area in the B2B or corporate space is being discussed? Want to know who the powerful voices are? Where are the critical channels and platforms? This is all information that is possible to glean through digital channels; helping us to plan content and campaigns and ensuring we put together targeted distribution plans.

As we have discussed already in previous chapters 3 and 4, the media industry is under incredible strain at the moment and this is even more the case in the B2B sector, where many industry publications have either massively scaled back or have even been forced to close. This information is still likely to exist but is now just as likely to be found on social networks, forums and LinkedIn Groups than it is via the traditional media. So, this opens up new opportunities for us to get our messages in front of the people that matter.

DEMONSTRATING VALUE THROUGH CONVERSION

While the role of websites and online destinations have shifted considerably within the consumer marketing space, these still play a pivotal role when it comes to B2B marketing. When the goal of a campaign is often to capture information or data that can be used by a sales team, for example, then digital channels provide a clear customer journey that can be tracked and optimised. Content is always a vital component here. Content marketing has been a buzzword for many years now but it is nothing new. The idea of providing content that is value-add to someone and using that as a door-opener to strike up a conversation about a product or service is hardly revolutionary. It is just that it is easier to do online.

All of the above discussion applies just as equally to the corporate PR space. Whether it is identifying themes or providing easy (or hard) to access information about a particular topic or business, digital channels are often more than adept at helping. The targeting options that are available are equally powerful when confronting a corporate PR objective. Often, there is a need to segment audiences – to craft different messages for different stakeholders depending on their interests and the angle they will be coming at the issue from.

Through tactics such as dark posting (where the content does not actually appear on your social feed but is instead just shown to the people that you select), you can now ensure that tailored messages reach the right people at the right time – a powerful way of mobilising support around a particular campaign or finding ways to minimise objections but answering the questions that are most pertinent to particular audience groups.

BUILDING REPUTATION

A central tenet of corporate PR is building, and preserving, reputation. It is also something that feeds into many consumer and B2B PR strategies. Increasingly, in this modern era, the secret to building reputation is to ensure you walk the walk and talk the talk. Often, this requires businesses to meaningfully act in a way that matches the corporate message they want to convey and a lot of this starts well away from communication strategies – digital or otherwise – and sits well within the business itself.

But, there is a role for digital PR to play in building reputation and much of it comes down not only to the content created – and distributed – but also the way that the business conveys itself. That can be anything from the way your website positions you – for example, are pictures of your people front and centre? Do you talk about your commitment to the environment or diversity? – to the way you speak through a tone of voice on your social channels. Are you a business that is highly responsive? Do you get back to enquiries quickly? Are you updating regularly and are you giving as much weight to things like corporate responsibility as you are about products, services and sales?

As mentioned earlier, a lot of this will start with a focus on who you are trying to reach. Where are your different stakeholder groups and what are the various messages that you want to convey to them?

DEVELOPING THOUGHT LEADERS

Another important part of building reputation – and often at the core of both corporate and B2B campaigns – is thought leadership. The first step of this is – as outlined earlier – to use available data to see what the relevant topics or issues are that you should be engaging with. This is actually a critical first step. Do the areas that are interesting to you as a business intersect and crossover with what your audience cares about? And, if so, what are the themes that matter? Who is speaking loudest and where are they speaking?

The process of building thought leaders within your business is now easier than ever. As we saw in the chapter 7 on influencers, digital channels give anyone the opportunity to build influence and a following. There are three components that dictate whether this is possible. The first is whether this person has authority to speak. It is not a given that this is required, but generally speaking, someone with a position of authority already will find it easier to build a presence online. So, identify the right people within your business that you believe have an authentic right to be speaking out on these subjects.

The second area to focus on is the content itself. I have seen many so-called 'thought leaders' really struggle. They might hold high-up positions within businesses – for example, the chief executive officer (CEO) – but the content they share is not compelling. Think about consumer-focused influencers – often, these are teenagers with no authority whatsoever, but because they can create compelling digital content that people want to consume, they are able to build up powerful and influential followings on their social channels.

The final aspect that is absolutely vital in my eyes is transparency. Again, to use the example of the CEO with plenty of authority, so often it is very clear that the CEO herself is nowhere near the Twitter account. It is clearly run by her PR team and the content feels staid and dull. Social channels in particular rely on personality. Of course, CEOs are busy people and there are always going to be ways for processes to be streamlined, but ensuring the thought leader is closely involved in his or her thought leadership strategy – and execution – is absolutely vital.

Once these components are in place, then it is worth thinking about channels and distribution. Your data analysis will be able to assist with the channel question – where are these conversations currently happening and, once identified, these are therefore the places where it makes sense for the thought leader to be active. When it comes to distribution – as in Chapter 9 – do not shy away from a range of distribution options including paid media. But, it is also important to remember that the most effective thought leadership distribution strategies rely on true engagement with the community. Engaging with other thought leaders, entering into real (even real life) debate and dialogue again shows a level of authenticity and will begin to build a true community around a topic or theme with the thought leader themselves embedded within it.

WORKING WITH WIKIPEDIA

There are obviously many channels that will have an impact or importance with a corporate or B2B PR campaign. But, one that has been a particular source of debate and often struggle within the industry is Wikipedia, and so it makes sense to just pause and spend a little bit of time interrogating this platform.

Wikipedia is a unique phenomenon. Launched in 2001, it now ranks as one of the most trusted sources on the internet and frequently will be one of the first search results that shows up.

Wikipedia not only shows the power of crowdsourcing, but also the perils. Created by the wisdom of the community, Wikipedia relies on volunteers to create and update all the site's content. Despite this, generally speaking, the accuracy and lack of bias on the platform is quite phenomenal. But, it is not perfect and this often causes challenges for individuals and brands – especially, around contentious issues.

Because of the unique nature of Wikipedia, changing or correcting information on the platform – even if quite clearly inaccurate – requires a similarly unique approach and centres on working with the community to resolve. As a rule of thumb, it is generally advisable to constantly monitor for changes that have been made to your brand or individual page on Wikipedia and check that you are satisfied with these changes or, at least, that they are accurate. Malicious attacks to pages are generally rare and tend to be reserved for high profile individuals, brands or situations.

When trying to correct information, make sure you have factual sources to prove your case. Under Wikipedia rules you are not permitted to make direct changes to a page where you have a direct business interest – and that means intermediaries, such as agencies, working on your behalf. You must use the community pages to make your case. It is worth remembering that you will often be conversing with a volunteer that will have a lot of changes to mediate and manage, so being polite and courteous is probably the best course of action and piece of advice when working with Wikipedia. Wikipedia has very clear rules and guidelines that lay out the process for escalating issues that are not resolved and, again, it is worth checking these before engaging as they do change from time to time.

Above all, remember that Wikipedia is an unbiased, encyclopaedic resource that aims to provide accurate information. It is not a vehicle for corporate spin and this is where brands and PR professionals usually come unstuck. As long as you remember this and abide by the community rules, Wikipedia should not cause any significant brand reputation for your brand or business.

MANAGING CRISIS

When a crisis happens, so often, digital channels – and social in particular – become the epicentre. Often, social media becomes the first red flag and the first alert that something is wrong. Which is yet another argument for the need to be constantly monitoring important keywords related to your business – from brand and products names to competitors and industry themes that might be pertinent. Ensuring that you have a grasp on what is being said about you could give you critical hours of advance notice of something before it all kicks off.

The reality is that crisis situations can stem from anywhere and digital provides many additional opportunities for things to go wrong. Community management is a case in point where many businesses have become unstuck over the last few years with rogue (or even well meaning) community managers landing a business in trouble.

But, there are plenty of opportunities for digital to play an important role in helping you manage a crisis – right from using social listening to provide an early warning to using things like dark sites to ensure you are ready to go with pre-defined messaging.

As with all forms of crisis communications – digital and non-digital – being prepared is absolutely key. There are two vital components here:

1. *Documentation* – Make sure that crisis plans – online and offline – have been clearly thought through. This includes

everything from escalation plans and contacts through to scenario planning. So often, these plans end up as weighty documents that just sit on a server somewhere collecting dust. Increasingly, I am encouraging businesses to think how they can be more flexible about how they present this information – for example, through a mobile app that anyone access anywhere, no matter when something kicks off, as the one thing most people are likely to have easy access to is their mobile phone.

2. *Practise* – And yet, the best documentation in the world does not mean that your business knows how it needs to act when a crisis happens. So, practising this through training and simulations is a great way to ensure the business is crisis-ready. Often, your community managers will be at the forefront of a crisis – so much better to have them practising in a safe, closed environment than practising in real-life when everything is kicking off. But, it is not just community managers who need to practise. Many people in your business – and it tends to be more senior people – do not always realise just how quickly you need to react to crises in a digital world. Legal teams and the C-suite who like to have hours and hours to perfect and sign-off a perfect statement will be shocked to realise that digital conversations will not wait for them. So, practise and make sure they know this up front.

There is a wealth of more sophisticated digital considerations that you might want to bear in mind. For example, do you own all web domains that might be used against you? Have you factored a search strategy into your crisis plans to ensure you are ready to intercept searches that might increase significantly if something hits the public eye? Have you factored in how you will use digital channels to interact with internal staff and influencers and advocates in times of crisis?

Digital has changed the voracity and speed of crisis situations. But digital also offers new opportunities to get ahead of a crisis and deal with it in the most effective way possible.

PUBLIC AFFAIRS AND LOBBYING

Politics is another area where digital has ushered in dramatic changes. Indeed, Member of Parliament (MP)s and political influencers are often some of the most enthusiastic users of digital communication channels. So, it stands to reason that any modern public affairs approach will effectively utilise a lot of the tactics and techniques we have talked about in this book so far.

Whether that is ensuring that target audiences and messages have been crafted with the right people in mind or ensuring that you are using effective paid media distribution to get the right messages in front of the right people. So, much of public affairs and lobbying can be benefited with a digital PR approach. Monitoring is another area that will add significant value. Keeping an eye on how politicians and the political elite are using social media to convey messaging will allow you to identify the areas that are being prioritised and ensuring you are reacting and acting on this insight accordingly.

INTERNAL COMMUNICATIONS AND EMPLOYEE ENGAGEMENT

Many will be familiar with the refrain 'your employees are your greatest communication asset' but it is only really recently that businesses have started to truly understand the potential of this and act on it. Digital channels have certainly turbo-charged this approach and communication to internal audiences and seeing them as an opportunity to engage wider stakeholders – especially, in B2B sectors – now seems to be coming of age, finally.

Let us take the latter first. I recently worked with a large multinational corporation. It worked in a highly regulated industry and for years; their social media guidelines to employees had basically been, 'don't talk about the company on social media'. They got a new CEO and he suddenly realised one day that this was a crazy policy. His employees were often highly skilled and had networks of people in exactly the target audiences that were important to them. They were missing out on a massive opportunity to engage this audience and could use their employees as a vehicle to do so. So, from that moment on he put in place an empowerment and training process – combined with smart technology – that has already started to pay dividends.

The empowerment point here is a crucial one. Often, the biggest barrier to true employee engagement is employees feeling as though they are not permitted to post on behalf of the business. Increasingly, we have seen a number of platforms emerge that allow you to create and distribute content to employees that they are then actively encouraged to use on their social platforms. These types of solutions have great potential but, alone, will not solve the issue. I have seen many examples where these platforms have been rolled out to great fanfare only to sit collecting dust.

That is because at the heart of this – like so many digital approaches – lies great content. And, for employees, it is likely to be different content to the sort of content you are sending out via owned channels or to other audiences. To encourage your employees to use their own social channels to share information about their employer, you need to provide them with content that they would be proud to share or, ideally, something that makes them look good.

ENTERPRISE SOCIAL NETWORKING

But, the use of digital channels in this space is not just to encourage employees to share outside the business, it is to encourage them to collaborate and discuss internally using digital channels and use this as an opportunity to provide them with relevant internal comms. This is another area that has been slow to take off but is finally showing signs of maturing. I remember talking to clients about Yammer over five years ago and helping to create best practice approaches that would aid take up within a business. It was a hard ask back then and remains a complex area, despite the fact that the technology has come some way.

Much of this is about 'ease'. Employees are busy and just putting more clutter into their lives without answering the 'what's in it for me' question is fruitless. You either need to make their lives easier or you need to provide them with content that informs or entertains, constantly. So often, I hear the argument that internal communication tools will help reduce email, but too often, that just never materialises. Our businesses are incredibly tied to email and removing these bonds will not happen overnight.

Thankfully, 'ease of use' is something that is beginning to come through the internal communication technologies that are out there. Take something like Workplace from Facebook. It is essentially a closed version of Facebook for your business. And, because it is an identical version of Facebook, the chances are a vast proportion of your workforce will already be familiar with it and know how to use it. This is just an example of how some adoption barriers can be pulled down. And, while creating engaging content for internal audiences is not easy, with the right time, focus and resources, it is certainly possible.

It is also worth flagging that technology will not always be the solution. Many internal audiences will not have easy access to technology – at least a computer. For example, those working in factory settings or in certain markets around the world. So, making sure you have covered all bases before embarking on your technology platform is important. And, if all else fails, do not forget some of the most basic forms of digital communication – such as short message service (SMS) – which could provide an easy solution.

QUESTIONS

1. Are you fully utilising digital PR for B2B comms?

2. How are you using targeting to identify audiences?

3. How can you be more granular in using data to inform insights?

4. Are you effectively building corporate brand reputation through your online PR efforts?

5. Who are your thought leaders? Have you established an effective digital footprint for them?

6. Do your thought leaders have something meaningful to say?

7. Are you monitoring for Wikipedia changes and updates to content relevant to you?

8. Are your community managers trained to deal with crisis situations?

9. Have you stress tested your digital crisis plan?

10. Are you properly making the most of the potential power of employees?

11. Are you empowering employees to act?

11

REPORTING AND MEASUREMENT

If there is one charge that has often been levelled at the PR industry in general, it is that it has always struggled with measurement. In addition, there is plenty of truth in this accusation. One of my favourite examples of this is case study videos where you see reach or impression figures for PR activity in the millions – or sometimes billions. Of course, this is all meaningless. Adding together newspaper circulation figures or online publication traffic numbers is as blunt an instrument as you can possibly get. It does not provide any insights and often, frankly, it is a lie. At best, it gives you a relative measure of the reach of a particular publication. Nevertheless, that is about it. It says nothing about the number of people that were exposed to an article, what they thought about it and/or what they did as a result. However, herein lies the rub. These are very difficult things to discern through traditional PR outputs.

The reality is that measurement of traditional PR is hard, especially in terms of linking back to real business impact. Because media publishers often own the resulting piece of 'coverage', it is difficult to collect useful data – whether offline or even online. While new approaches such as brand tracking studies can help demonstrate the power of PR activities, it is not a perfect tool as it is often hard to split out different marketing activities and attribution is never entirely accurate. However, it is a start.

BATTLING A BAD REPUTATION

It is not as though the industry has not been trying. The work of the International Association for the Measurement and Evaluation of Communication (AMEC), in particular, has made incredible progress and has been tireless in raising the awareness of issues around the measurement of PR and communications. Their oft-cited treatise, The Barcelona Principles (AMEC, 2016), is an important stake in the ground that sets out the key tenets of any effective PR measurement approach:

- Goal setting and measurement are fundamental to communication and public relations.

- Measuring communication outcomes is recommended versus only measuring outputs.

- The effect on organisational performance can and should be measured where possible.

- Measurement and evaluation require both qualitative and quantitative methods.

- Advertising value equivalents (AVE) are not the value of communication.

- Social media can and should be measured consistently with other media channels.

- Measurement and evaluation should be transparent, consistent and valid.

AMEC's focus in particular on demonstrating the absolute flaw of the AVE metric has been particularly welcome. Of a long list of failings that AVEs encompass, the fundamental one is that the PR industry needs to assert its true value and merely comparing it to traditional advertising is a poor way to achieve that.

Thankfully, digital PR offers new opportunities that will finally begin to put effective measurement within reach for PR practitioners.

SETTING OBJECTIVES

It always sounds ludicrously silly, but the reality is that most of the challenges around measurement can be solved – or at least simplified – by setting clear objectives from the outset. It is incredible how few PR campaigns manage to achieve this. In the brief should be a clearly stated objective for the particular piece of activity that is to be undertaken. Ideally, there should be one central objective with other supporting ones nestled underneath as needed.

There are many reasons why setting objectives is important; however, when it comes to measurement, the main one is that if you do not set clear objectives then how are you ever going to be able to put in place key performance indicators (KPIs) that establish whether you've been successful or not?

Not all objectives are created equal and where possible, they need to be specific. Simply writing the word 'awareness' makes it very difficult to work out how to measure success. Awareness with whom? Where? How? With what message? This is the level of detail that is needed to really crystallise 'what good looks like'. Setting this clarity up front is vital – it is amazing how often these sorts of things are post rationalised after the horse has bolted.

THE RIGHT STRATEGY

The next steps to successful digital PR measurement lie in the strategy. In addition, more specifically, it lies in the campaign planning. Take an example. Say you have a campaign and the primary objective is all around generating website clicks to a landing page. A piece of offline PR coverage is going to be pretty impossible to measure whether the objective has been met. Whereas, some social content with paid media optimised for web clicks, with short codes on the links to track the traffic, is going to be far easier to demonstrate success.

Again, it all seems pretty straightforward, but it is always surprising to see campaigns that are built in a way that makes it impossible to measure against the set objectives. Of course, it is clear to see how this is possible if objectives were not set from the outset.

Therefore, when planning campaigns, measurement needs to be baked in. What is the audience journey? How will they see content? What do we want them to do with it? Moreover, how will we know if they have done it? If we cannot answer these types of questions then the strategy probably has not been developed effectively. Collaboration is a core component here. Making sure that strategists and analysts/measurement experts are working together during campaign planning is an important way to ensure that effective measurement will be possible. Too often, measurement is an afterthought once a campaign is completed, rather than being something that is strategically considered at the outset. Good strategists will be able to cover this off in their planning work.

FINDING AND COLLECTING DATA

If the objectives and strategy have been properly thought through, then finding and collecting data should be relatively easy. Once you have your strategic approach laid out, you can start to identify the points at which you will be able collect data and what that data looks like.

Obviously, a key consideration here is the tools that you might need in order to collect the data and whether there are any technical elements here that need to be factored in. For example, making sure you have tracking pixels on websites or landing pages to track traffic and where it has come from. Many of these considerations need to be included from the start; thus, making sure this planning work has been done will save a lot of time and stress further down the line.

The good news is that most of the tools out there these days are pretty powerful; whether that is more traditional solutions like website analytics, or the native analytics platforms that are included with most of the key social networks. Where possible, find ways to validate the data: for example, to ensure you have an accurate read, consider using more than one tool to ensure accuracy.

DROWNING IN DATA AND KPIS

It is equally the great thing about digital, and a potential peril as well, that everything (or most things) is measurable. I have seen some pretty meaty digital reports in my time. Page after page of datapoints that have been collected. However, most of it is pretty meaningless and tells you nothing. Data must not be used as proof points in itself, only if it provides insights.

That is why KPIs are absolutely vital. Once the strategic approach has been decided and defined, one can then identify the KPIs that should be put against each part of the campaign. Ideally, there should only be one KPI for each element and, generally speaking, the fewer the better. The more you have, the more resource intensive and the more chance that you will miss something important because you are being blinded by datapoints.

Yes, there is a lot that we can measure, but the idea behind KPIs is to really focus on what we *should* measure.

The other really important aspect of KPIs is that they should be relative measures. A KPI is not a metric. A metric is a measure of something – for example, the number of people arriving at a website. A KPI is a measurable value that demonstrates whether you are meeting a certain objective – for example, month-on-month comparison of website traffic. Knowing what your social media engagement rate is is one thing. Knowing that it is beating your target or average is a KPI. The two are easily confused but are fundamentally different.

OUTPUTS AND OUTCOMES

As we saw in the Barcelona Principles earlier, there is a difference between measuring outputs and outcomes and one is much more valuable than the other. It is easy to see how measuring outputs is something that we all become obsessed by: how many press releases did we write this month? How many social media posts did we send out? These are all measures of efficiency or quantity; are we doing stuff?

However, there is really no point in measuring this is we are not also measuring what this 'stuff' has achieved – is it working? Is it helping us meet our business objectives? Should we still be doing it?

Again, it is a pretty easy concept but it is amazing how often the two are confused or how often the former is present and the latter is absent. It is easy to justify the success of a person or a team on their outputs; however, it is much harder to assess their outputs based on the outcomes that they have generated. Moreover, that is probably why often it just does not happen.

COVERAGE TRACKING

The other most common metric that exists within the PR industry is measurement of coverage, as we have already discussed. When we looked previously at the state of the media and the new media ecosystem that now exists, driven by digital channels, we saw that actually, these days, coverage alone is not enough. You might get a great hit on a national newspaper website, but if the publication did not post the article on its Facebook page (with millions of followers) then is it still a success?

I have seen examples where two seemingly identical pieces of coverage have been shared with a client as part of a coverage round-up. The way this coverage was reported to the client made it seem as though the two pieces were equally as effective. However, what was not shared in the round-up was that one was distributed extensively by the publisher in question through social media, generating over 500 shares. The other wasn't at all. This is a great example of how we often do not tell the full story – especially, when it comes to coverage in the sophisticated media landscape that we see today. Where sharing coverage and reporting on its effectiveness, we need to make sure we have a clear picture of how coverage has travelled and how stories have been distributed – or not – and be really honest with ourselves about whether something was a success or not.

A REVOLUTION IN SOCIAL MEASUREMENT

It is only in traditional PR where the rulebook is gradually shifting. In social media too, as more and more advertising revenue starts to flow in, there is more and more focus on metrics that matter. For a sector that has long focused on engagement as a key success metric, more questions are being asked and more focus on whether engagement on its own actually means anything.

Again, all of this comes back to our initial premise of understanding your objective and strategic approach. Engagement might be a KPI that suggests whether, relatively speaking, content is performing but it is unlikely to be the ultimate judge of whether something has been successful at impacting the bottom line.

Social media have an advantage here. With more and more focus by the social networks around building features and formats that lead to conversion, there is more opportunity to build campaigns that do result in something meaningful and measurable. As social commerce continues to expand, these opportunities will only increase.

DASHBOARDS AND REPORTS

As mentioned earlier, when it comes to digital, there is always a temptation to blind with metrics. Reports that include every datapoint under the sun are now commonplace and are largely useless. It always suggests that objectives and KPIs have not been properly defined. A much braver option is to identify the two or three KPIs that really matter and focus there. Not only does this ensure that everything is objective-aligned, but it is also much easier for key stakeholders to digest.

Although many businesses will still dictate that reports are delivered on a weekly or monthly basis and that often this ends up being static reports, there is a general trend now towards real-time dashboards that provide snapshots of how activity is performing. This is now a relatively straightforward process to setup. Data in the digital space is usually available in close to real-time and most platforms now provide open Application Programming Interface (APIs) that allow you to pull different data sources together and present them in a unified way in one dashboard.

Not only does this become less resource-intensive (after an initial setup) than collating static reports, but also makes sure the data is available to view at any time. The problem with monthly – or, for some businesses, even weekly – reports is that if you are always waiting for the report before you take action, then often you might have missed the opportunity to affect change and tweak or optimise an approach. Of course, providing a real-time dashboard still does not guarantee that anyone will actually look at it, but it does then give you more opportunity to build insight and conclusions that can be shared rather than putting this same resource into report creation.

MAKING IT MATTER – USING LEARNINGS AND INSIGHTS

Speaking of which, at the end of the day, data is just data. It's meaningless without analysis and the analysis is pretty useless unless it is actionable. That's one of the problems with large-scale reports with thousands of datapoints – these usually get circulated and then filed – often unread. No recommendations are made and no action is taken to optimise. That pretty much renders the whole exercise useless. Every measurement approach should be working towards providing insight – and the best insights are ones that tell you something you do not know; something you can change.

That could be a wholesale strategic shift – understanding that the approach is not right and needs to be changed.

On the other hand, it could be something that is far more agile. It could be seeing that a piece of content is not performing as expected and so either needs to be changed or tweaked or even stopped entirely. This is particularly applicable when looking at the social media space. These real-time optimisations will become an increasing part of any form of digital campaigning but insights are necessary across the board. Yearly planning and budgets are too often formed on a copy and paste process based on what happened the year before. However, using real insight on how activities have performed previously is a critical way of ensuring that PR activities – whether digital or otherwise – are really playing a value-add role for a business, which, above anything else, will be the best way to guarantee the role of communications within a business.

QUESTIONS

1. Are you still measuring using over-inflated impression figures?

2. Do your campaigns have clear measurable objectives?

3. Do our strategy and approach make effective measurement possible?

4. Are you able to effectively collect the data necessary to prove Return On Investment (ROI)?

5. Do you know the right datapoints to use?

6. Are you meeting the requirements of the Barcelona Principles?

7. Are you measuring outputs *and* outcomes?

8. If you are only measuring the quantity of coverage, how can you add more specific metrics to support this?

9. Are you using real-time dashboards and reports to make measurement more agile and useful?

10. Are you taking learnings from reports and using them to improve activity?

12

EMERGING TECHNOLOGY

The challenge with writing a book about digital technology is that it is often out of date as soon as the last word is typed, let alone printed. Therefore, with this in mind, writing a chapter on emerging technology is always in danger of starting with defeat. Thus, rather than trying to detail all the technologies that are emerging now – and could be in the future – the idea of this chapter is to give an overview of how to approach and embrace emerging technologies, that is, what to look out for and how to make the right choices. It is not a blow-by-blow account of whether Augmented Reality (AR) or Virtual Reality (VR) is likely to be more beneficial for your business. We are living in a technologically driven world and some of the innovations that will happen over the next 10 years are beyond our current comprehension.

This is such an incredibly fast industry. If you think that just over 10 years ago, no one, apart from Apple engineers, had heard of the iPhone. Twitter did not exist and Facebook did, but only just. The pace of change that we now experience is unlike any other. In addition, this poses great challenges for those of us working in business. How do we decide where to place our bets and where to pass? Marketing and communication has equal challenges. With marketing technology alone, you will likely receive inbound sales enquiries on a regular basis offering you some sort of new social listening tool or other. It would be a full-time job to constantly keep abreast of these technological changes. In addition, often, the reality is they are all much of a muchness. Moreover, that is before we even get into the most innovative technologies that we might consider using to make campaigns more effective.

Therefore, this is an area that the traditional PR professional just did not have to tackle. However, these days it is a reality of the world in which we work.

HOW TO USE TECHNOLOGY

Technology is everywhere. Much like digital in PR, it is often impossible to divorce technology from our daily lives. This is absolutely true when it comes to the use of technology in marketing and communications. This whole book has been written on the subject. Everything we do, from campaign planning through to delivery and measurement, is now driven by and aided by technology.

It is probably areas such as data collection and analysis where the use of technology is most obvious. In addition, there is significant progress being made here. If you can utilise approaches such as artificial intelligence and automation to streamline and reduce human interaction in pulling together things like monthly reports then that is a business efficiency worth doing. When building teams – as we shall see in Chapter 13 – identifying where technology can play a meaningful role is important to factor in.

Another area that is ripe for technological innovation is in marketing and communication process. Traditionally, the PR industry has been slow to adopt processes such as project management. However, tools in this space will really help drive additional efficiency as well increase effectiveness through collaboration.

It is not just in these more obvious areas where technology is playing a role. Increasingly, technology is pushing the creative product, too. You only need to look at recent winners at the annual Cannes Lions Festival of Creativity to see that technology is often interwoven into the 'big idea'. Technology can offer rich new storytelling opportunities – a way to grab an audience in fresh new ways or uncover new approaches to distributing that story.

Finally, it is worth just acknowledging – as we have throughout this book – that increasingly technology powers the way we distribute content. Either through platforms like social networks or through the devices we use to consume content – whether mobile device or not – increasingly, devices in our homes are 'smart' and voice-controlled.

AVOIDING THE BANDWAGON

If, like me, you are a bit of a technology geek at heart that just cannot get enough of digital innovation, then you will be familiar with the constant battle raging over whether to utilise new technologies or not. I have seen many campaigns where the idea clearly rests on a piece of technology and the creative has probably been put together with that piece of technology in mind. The idea serves the technology.

Then, you have what I'd call gimmick marketing, where a brand comes out with a new innovation using newly released technology just to get some headlines. It usually comes hot on the heels of the new technology itself being announced and, unfortunately, often picks up a range of awards as a result.

For some brands, where telling an innovation story is important then these approaches can often make sense. However, in many cases, it just feels like desperation. Rather, technology innovation should be used to make the idea better – whether making it more creatively impactful, more efficient or more effective in achieving bottom-line results. This is easier said than done and the above-mentioned pitfalls are easy to fall into.

One of the sure-fire ways to stay on the right side of using innovation within campaigns is to first ensure that you have a clear overview of what is out there. Again, easier said than done. In the digital world, innovation occurs constantly. Thus, staying abreast of the latest developments is not easy. However, it is important. Only by having a clear idea of what is out there can you most effectively identify opportunities within campaigns or ongoing activities that can be improved as a result.

There is often a trend towards hiring individuals or building teams that focus on innovation. In addition, it is easy to see, with the fast-paced nature of the digital world in mind, why this is a tempting thing to do. However, I have never really seen this approach work successfully. In addition, that is because you need to embed this knowledge into teams. Much better to have a creative, for example, that understands the latest technologies and can seamlessly embed rather than having an innovation specialist trying to come in and sprinkle innovation fairy dust over existing programmes and activities.

TRIAL AND ERROR

One of the biggest barriers to adoption of innovation is fear of failure. When faced with something tried and tested and something new and untested, the former most generally wins out. Most budgeting still works like this, for example. You take your budget from last year; you tweak it a bit, but it basically remains the same. Finding ways to jolt you out of this stasis in a way that feels safe is therefore key.

That is where pilot programmes can really add value. Rather than putting all your eggs into one basket, identify an area you want to innovate in and identify a way to 'pilot' this on a small scale before rolling out more widely. This is much easier to do in the digital realm than it would have been previously. Generally, it is easier to run smaller scale programmes – for example, siphoning off a small proportion of paid media budget to put into something new and untested.

Another useful framework that can be adopted for campaigns an ongoing activity – as we have already discussed – is the 70/20/10 model. This is a model that is often attributed to Google (Forbes, 2011), and the way they set their teams up for innovation.

In the Google model, employees were encouraged to spend 70% of their time on their day jobs, 20% of their time working with another team to bring fresh perspective and 10% of their time on something totally new. I think this is a very useful model to use in digital PR to encourage innovation. You accept that 70% of your campaign or ongoing activity is going to be tried and tested approaches that are proven to work. You then commit 20% to innovating on what you already have – thus, maybe a split test on a piece of content. In addition, then you ring-fence 10% to try something totally new that you have never done before.

The theory behind this suggests that you can be more calculated in your approach rather than throwing caution to the wind. Of course, the hope is that the 10% of true innovation will prove itself and you will then be able to make that – or part of it – the 70% next time round, but it will be based on a tried and tested pilot. Obviously, if the 10% does not work then at least you know and you are safe in the knowledge that you have only wasted 10% of your budget or resources on it.

PROVING RETURN ON INVESTMENT (ROI)

The other benefit that digital piloting brings is the ability to test and measure results to prove the business case and demonstrate why scaling is worthwhile. It is one thing to be able to say you think a particular innovation is worth investing in. It is another to be able to prove it and back it up with data.

One of the keys to success in being able to prove the value is to be very clear from the outset what 'good' looks like. As we covered in the chapter 11 on measurement, it is important to have a clear picture on what your objective is. When it comes to innovation, this alone is not enough. You also need to be clear on what you feel this innovation will do to add value. In addition, that might be different to the overall objective. Sure, it might demonstrate tangible improvements on the KPIs of the particular campaign. However, it could also perform other returns, such as driving budget efficiencies or doing something in a more streamlined way.

It is then important that you put in place a strategy and measurement framework that allows you to collect the necessary data to prove that the innovation has worked. It is amazing how many pilots end with inconclusive results: 'if only we'd measured XYZ'. It is always hard to predict what these unknowns will be, but it is vital.

It is also worth bearing in mind the stakeholders that will ultimately be looking at this innovation and judging whether it is worth embracing and continuing with. How can you ensure that the way the results are presented and packaged will be a persuasive business case that will demonstrate real value? Again, when it comes to doing new things, the easiest state is to do nothing. Therefore, to convince someone of the opposite, you need to work twice as hard.

THE COMMUNICATION OPPORTUNITY IN TECHNOLOGY

We touched earlier on the dangers of using technology as an excuse to get a good PR story, but it is wrong to see this as purely a negative. Often technology and innovation are important consumer or corporate brand-building opportunities and should be viewed as strategically important. In the past, digital innovations were really the domain of technology companies. However, these days, every company is really a technology company, though some are better than others.

Demonstrating why your technological innovations will improve your business – either through revenue gains, efficiencies or better customer service – is often a very positive move. However, there are other areas where it will also come into play.

Talent is a good example. The talent battle is fierce. If you feel your business would be improved with more effective technology, then how are you going to fight the likes of Google and Facebook for the best talent? It will not be easy.

Therefore, as we go on to think about how PR teams now operate within a business, it is worth remembering that technology is not a silo anymore. It is not the territory of the IT department; it is something that is now as fundamental to a business as electricity or water. Technology drives businesses and organisations forward and communicating this is now often business critical. As communicators, we need to be constantly on the lookout for how technology can improve the work we do, and how we can tell the story about the technology that our businesses, or the businesses we represent, are utilising every day to succeed and thrive.

QUESTIONS

1. What are the processes you currently undertake that could benefit from technology?

2. How are you using technology to aid creativity and storytelling?

3. How are you embedding innovation across your team or comms function?

4. Can you` use 70/20/10 thinking to help constant innovation?

5. How can you use technology to tell a brand innovation story?

6. Do you have the right talent to make true innovation work? What is missing?

13

BUILDING A FUTURE-PROOFED
PR TEAM

Digital ushers forth so many opportunities for our industry. However, to properly adapt to a digital age, we need to change and change fast – both in agencies and in-house. The real challenge here is that, in so many ways, PR is an industry that is not easily positioned to make the most of digital. We have seen that time and time again throughout this book, but it is probably most evident when we consider how PR teams are formed and operate – both traditionally but also in the new world we are encountering.

PR is a discipline that is built on people. Pitching to a journalist relies, to a surprisingly large extent, on the persuasive powers of one person to another. I have often seen two people pitch the same story and get a significantly different outcome. The PR industry – in-house and agency – has been built upon a generalist model. You have individuals that are storytellers, pitchers and analysts rolled into one. On the agency side, these people are expected to manage clients and projects, too. In addition, that model has hardly shifted. Contrast that – in particular, in the agency-world – to advertising or digital marketing industries where specialist teams are pulled together with different skill sets and knowledge bases.

Suddenly, the rise of digital has made the generalist's life a whole load harder. And then throw in all the new specialisms we have covered in this book – digital content, social networks, data, paid media, search and digital marketing. The list goes on. Suddenly, you have a situation where even the best practitioner would struggle to perform everything brilliantly on top of their existing PR knowledge.

That is not to say there is no value in breadth of knowledge and, in many ways, that is the wonderful aspect of the PR industry that I feel we must preserve. However, I believe to truly succeed, we need to embrace depth of specialism, too. In addition, that is often a challenge. Increasingly, we need to embrace T-shaped people – those that not only have a broader knowledge and understanding of context, but also have a deep knowledge in a particular area and how that area contributes to the larger whole.

STARTING FROM SCRATCH

So how do we transform? I used to spend quite a bit of time working in the technology sector and with startups, in particular. Startups have one major advantage (also, something very scary) over other businesses – they are starting from a blank sheet of paper. They can build teams from scratch rather than feeling as though they are having to base everything on a legacy structure. It is a pretty exciting position to be in and, in one of these cases, I was helping the head of communication to build a team to support such a business. She had a headcount of four people and this is who we ended up hiring:

- *Copywriter* - He was an ex-journalist so understood how to craft a story, but could also pitch. He also had good experience in the social space and thus could cover off writing copy for social and digital channels.

- *Maker* – Very deliberately not a designer; she was a multi-talented person who was able to design assets but could also do simple video editing. She was a great photographer and understood how a story could come to life through multimedia channels.

- *Analyst* – A great data strategist, but someone who could also manage paid media campaigns on social; was great at pulling insights but also able to deliver reports that linked everything back to an ROI for the business.

- *Project manager* – Someone who made the trains run on time; kept the team together in an agile way and managed the agencies; in addition, was used to help with community management and other tasks that fell between the cracks.

The business then leaned on the agency I worked for to support with deeper resources in each of these areas as needed and to provide longer-term strategic guidance – for example, strategic planning and larger campaign delivery.

The team operated very well and as it grew; it mainly grew in these four areas – building a team out under each. I have always remembered this example as it felt like such a refreshing way to approach the situation. Thus, while many businesses are unlikely to have the opportunity to take a blank sheet of paper in exactly this way, it is a useful exercise. If you were starting out fresh with a headcount similar to the number of people in your team, how would you split up the roles and specialisms in a way that is different to what you currently have?

Then, how can you take your current hiring approach and mould it to get to a situation that is closer to your ideal over 12–24 months?

CRITICAL SKILLS

As the example above shows, there are different skill sets that are now needed. These can be broadly split into the following areas:

- *Data* – A wide ranging area (as seen in Chapter 2) that can cover data insight, performance analytics right the way through to measurement.

- *Strategy* – Again, can be broad, from brand strategy (more in agencies) through to media and campaign strategy; can also include specialists in sector knowledge or experts in crisis management or reputation.

- *Creative (agency)* – Taken from the world of the ad agency and more likely to be found in an agency setting.

- *Content production* – Whether it is all-round makers as in the case above or specialists in design or video production, this is a skill that is being increasingly needed across the board.

- *Copywriting* – Still at the heart of great PR activity – storytelling. Increasingly, these people will need to be able to write for a number of different formats and channels.

- *PR management/project management* – With projects and campaigns increasingly complex, having someone that can manage everything and keep it on track, is increasingly important. In an in-house environment, this might also be covered by a PR manager or brand manager – someone that would also be responsible for agency management and internal liaison.

- *Account management (agency)* – An agency skill that focuses on being the key day-to-day contact for a client.

- *Community management* – A crucial skill for social media activity and one that is probably more relevant than ever given the social shifts towards social networks acting more as active communities these days.

- *Media relations* – Still a mainstay of the PR discipline. Increasingly, this person needs to understand how the media is adapting and changing and this role may well merge with some of the skills mentioned above (e.g. account/project management or copywriting).

- *Digital production* – Often different from content production, this could cover everything from web or mobile development teams to those working with technologies such as AI or VR/AR.

- *Paid media* – Finally, as we start to use more and more paid media, agencies and in-house teams are beginning to require the services of someone that understands paid media in a more in-depth way.

There are other more specialist roles that might play a part depending on your focus and/or the areas that are relevant for your agency or business sector – for example, influencer marketing, SEO/PPC, reputation management or crisis management.

Moreover, not all of the above-mentioned skills will be relevant for every in-house team or for every agency. In addition, on the in-house side, it is obviously possible to outsource the above to an agency. I know many businesses that are making more use of agencies to help them juggle the various different specialisms they require – liking the fact that they can switch specialisms on and off as required. However, I have also seen some businesses who are seeing this as an opportune moment to bring new people and skill sets into their business directly and, in turn, reduce their agency reliance.

It is also important to stress that not all of these skills will always fall within the remit of a comms or PR team. Paid media, for example, will often be covered by a marketing team or a media agency. However, even in these situations, having someone that is conversant in it and is able to manage and oversee, will be of significant benefit.

FIXING THE SKILLS GAP

As discussed, changing this talent mix overnight will never be easy. Thus, sometimes, the best approach is to look for the gaps. How have outputs changed and where are you now lacking knowledge and skills? How can you make the case for new hires in new positions that might begin to demonstrate change in the right direction? The blank sheet of paper exercise helps in this regard because you can use it as a way to ensure you stay on the right track (though be aware how quickly things will change in a short period, so keep on refreshing the plan).

It is also worth thinking about where you can combine roles. In the startup example above, we combined paid media and data, for example. In smaller teams and in smaller agencies, you will not be able to have dedicated people or teams in every area; thus, where are the overlaps and how can you structure things around them?

Then, there is the team you already have. Where are the skills gaps and where is the opportunity for the existing team to be upskilled?

MANAGING INTERNAL SILOS

For in-house teams (though it is a challenge that agencies have to overcome too), the elephant in the room is often the role of the communication or PR team versus marketing/

digital/social/brand. I truly believe that in time these silos will begin to disperse and eventually disappear. Social and digital will (or should) be the first to go as these two areas begin to morph across everything. However, the role of PR versus other disciplines will always be a barrier to reshaping teams.

In a sense, the debate is a fruitless one and the faster all these disciplines can be seen as contributing to the broader whole, the better. However, in the meantime, the best solution is to agree the roles and responsibilities. Crucially, it is important to know the channels and approaches that are the responsibility of each team.

Then, it is worth looking at where certain specialisms (previously mentioned) can be shared across the marcomms function – for example, one analytics or production team that services all parts rather than building separate teams that do not ladder up together. Obviously, agencies will play a role in terms of providing resources in these areas but, even here, it is important to identify where there might be overlap. There is no point in reinventing the wheel several times. Integration and efficiency is the name of the game.

BRINGING NEW TALENT INTO AGENCIES

Agencies should be the place where this is easier to bring to fruition; however, agencies are also places where traditional structures are the most entrenched. The idea of the generalist PR professional in PR agencies – where they go from managing the client one minute to writing a press release and pitching to the media the next – is starting to rapidly unravel as the demands start to increase.

The traditional career path within a PR agency – rising from account executive through the ranks is incompatible with the range of demands and skill sets that are now required.

There are lots of different solutions that various leading agencies have put into practice, and here is not the place to cover them all. However, although there is no clear tried and tested approach to endorse, there is no doubt that the PR agency structure of the future will be one that embraces specialists in a way more similar to that of an advertising or digital agency.

My one key area of caution is to ensure the baby is not thrown out with the bathwater. As I have said numerous times, the PR approach is still incredibly valid in this day and age, so finding a way to stay true to the values of PR while still bringing in digital skills is a balance that is hard but vital.

SMALL CONSULTANCIES AND THE POWER OF PARTNERSHIP

In addition, this shift is hardest for smaller agencies. I started my career in agencies that are a fraction of the size of the one I work for today. In these smaller agencies, it is hard with smaller headcount to bring in the range of skill sets that larger agencies can. Thus, focusing on what will make the biggest impact is vital. In addition, staying true to your area of specialism is equally important. The blank sheet of paper exercise will help and in many ways the startup example given above is a good marker of where the answers may lie.

Another area to consider here is partnerships. Whether this is an informal arrangement between two or more smaller sized agencies or a more formal one, it is hard to advise without knowing the exact situation. However, finding ways to be able to offer clients integrated solutions without overreaching and hiring too many new skills is important to finding a manageable way forward. Partnerships with agencies that can offer complementary services is a tried and tested route for many looking to provide clients with a more rounded service offering.

TOOLS AND PROCESSES

Bringing new skills into a business is an incredibly exciting and a potentially game-changing initiative, whether in-house or agency. However, it almost always ushers in complexity and a wealth of new challenges. Generalist models are often easier to manage – relatively small teams are able to operate in an agile way that is often highly streamlined. Trying to do the same when the sheer number of people involved is greater is of course always going to be a challenge.

It will require an internal change. Communicating this and having a clear rationale will be vital for ensuring the existing and new workforce remains motivated. However, it will also require new working processes, tools and technologies. Some of this will be evolutions of what exist but some will be brand new. Again, we should look at the digital world for guidance here. It is worth looking at process methodologies such as Agile to see how fast-paced working can still exist with larger, more complex teams. There is also an opportunity here to build in efficiencies in the way teams work and communicate with each other. However, entering into this arena with eyes open in terms of the additional demands will ensure that these efficiencies are maximised and that the new, added complexity does not overwhelm or cause blockages.

BUILDING DIVERSITY

Finally, it would not be possible to talk about the PR team of the future without touching on diversity. It is a key area that is getting a lot of publicity and traction right now. It is my belief that the more diverse your team, the better your output will be. That is not only diversity in terms of gender and ethnicity, but also in terms of experience and talent.

Ultimately, we work in a business where we are communicating to an end audience. We have a responsibility to ensure that our output is as suitable for that audience as it possibly can be. That does not mean that we all need to reflect the audience we are communicating to, but it will certainly help if we can bring diverse points of view that will challenge and optimise.

QUESTIONS

1. Are you a generalist or a specialist team?

2. If you could start from scratch, what would your team look like?

3. What are the critical skills you need in your team? Where will you find them?

4. Where do partners or agencies have a role to play?

5. What are the tools and processes you need to make your team function?

6. How can you commit to talent diversity?

FURTHER READING

Ahmed, A. (2012). *Velocity*. London: Vermillion.

Godin, S. (2005). *Purple cow*. London: Penguin.

Godin, S. (2008). *Tribes*. New York, NY: Piatkus.

Harrison, S. (2016). *How to write better copy*. London: Bluebird.

Lewis, M. (2017). *The undoing project*. London: Penguin.

Levine, R., Locke, C., Weinberger, D., & Searls, D. (1999).*The cluetrain manifesto*. New York, NY: Basic Books

Li, C., & Bernoff, J. (2011). *Groundswell, expanded and revised edition: Winning in a world transformed by social technologies*. Cambridge, MA: Harvard Business Review Press.

Mele, N. (2013). *The end of big*. London: St. Martin's Press.

Pariser, E. (2012). *The filter bubble: How the new personalized web is changing what we read and how we think*. London: Penguin.

Rogers, D. (2015). *Campaigns that shook the world*. London: Kogan Page.

Singleton, A. (2014). *The PR masterclass*. London: Wiley.

Solomon, R. (2016). *The art of client service: The classic guide, updated for today's marketers and advertisers*. London: Wiley.

Steel, J. (1998). *Truth, lies, and advertising: The art of account planning.* London: Wiley.

Sterne, J. (2010). *Social media metrics: How to measure and optimize your marketing investment.* London: Wiley.

Waddington, S. (2012). *Share this.* London: Wiley.

REFERENCES

AMEC. (2016). Resource centre. Retrieved from https://amecorg.com/resource-centre/. Accessed on June 25, 2018.

ASA. (2017, August 21). Blog: Online influencers – Is it an #ad? Retrieved from https://www.asa.org.uk/news/online-influencers-is-it-an-ad.html. Accessed on June 25, 2018.

BBC News Labs. (2017, September 17). Beyond 800 words: New digital story formats for news. Retrieved from https://medium.com/bbc-news-labs/beyond-800-words-new-digital-story-formats-for-news-ab9b2a2d0e0d. Accessed on June 25, 2018.

Campaign. (2017, January 30). Procter & Gamble chief issues powerful media transparency rallying cry. Retrieved from https://www.campaignlive.co.uk/article/procter-gamble-chief-issues-powerful-media-transparency-rallying-cry/1422599. Accessed on June 25, 2018.

Facebook Newsroom. (2007, November 6). Facebook unveils Facebook Ads. Retrieved from https://newsroom.fb.com/news/2007/11/facebook-unveils-facebook-ads/. Accessed on June 25, 2018.

Fast Company. (2016, February 16). How BuzzFeed's Jonah Peretti is building a 100-year media company. Retrieved from https://www.fastcompany.com/3056057/how-buzzfeeds-jonah-peretti-is-building-a-100-year-media-company. Accessed on July 25, 2018.

Forbes. (2011, July 16). Google's innovation – And everyone's? Retrieved from https://www.forbes.com/ sites/quentinhardy/2011/07/16/googles-innovation-and-everyones/#4975d2d83066. Accessed on July 25, 2018.

Reuters Institute. (2017). Digital news report 2017. Retrieved from https://reutersinstitute.politics.ox.ac.uk/sites/ default/files/Digital%20News%20Report%202017%20 web_0.pdf. Accessed on June 25, 2018.

The Telegraph. (2017, October 8). Buzzfeed UK doubles turnover but losses rise on the back of rapid expansion. Retrieved from http://www.telegraph.co.uk/ business/2017/10/08/buzzfeeduk-doubles-turnover-205m-losses-top-35m/. Accessed on July 25, 2018.

USA Today. (2016, November 3). Mark Zuckerberg talks up Facebook's 'video first' strategy. Retrieved from https://www. usatoday.com/story/tech/news/2016/11/02/mark-zuckerberg-talks-facebook-video-first/93206596/. Accessed on June 25, 2018.

INDEX